HIDDEN MAN

By the same author

SURVIVAL OF DEATH

LIVING ON

HIDDEN MAN

PAUL BEARD

PILGRIM  BOOKS
TASBURGH   NORWICH   ENGLAND

British Library Cataloguing in Publication Data
Beard, Paul
  Hidden man.
  1. Self-realization   2. Psychical research
  I. Title
  131   BF637.S4

ISBN 0–946259–16–X

Photoset by Waveney Typesetters, Norwich
and printed in Great Britain by Oxford University Press

CONTENTS

	Acknowledgements	ix
1	A choice of horizon	1
2	The coming of the teacher	13
3	Continuous learning	31
4	Multi-levelled man	49
5	Entry into the inner world	64
6	Reincarnation	83
7	Reincarnation: an example	93
8	A glimpse into the group soul	105
9	Some parameters	117

With deep thanks to

Charles, Douglas, Elizabeth,
Ena, Estelle, Geraldine, Gladys,
Grace, Ivy, Kathleen, Marie, Maurice, Winifred

and others whose dedication
points a way for many.

ACKNOWLEDGEMENTS

My thanks are due to the following authors and publishers who have kindly acceded to my request to make quotations from the following:

The Rev. John Polkinghorne, F.R.S. and *The Times* for the article *The Search for Understanding*, printed on 18th February 1984.

The Society for Psychical Research, *Journal*, June 1945.

The Lucis Press: statement made by The Tibetan, and printed in the majority of the books of Alice A. Bailey.

The Psychic Press; Silver Birch teachings.

Violet Rutter: *Teachings of the Mandarin* (privately printed).

White Eagle Lodge; printed and private teachings of White Eagle.

Jane Roberts: The After-death Journal of an American Philosopher, Copyright 1978 by Jane Roberts, Prentice-Hall Inc., Englewood Cliffs, New Jersey, U.S.A.

Wm. Collins Sons & Co. Ltd.: *Swan in the Evening*, Rosamond Lehmann.

Hodder & Stoughton Ltd.: Dean Matthews, quoted in *Chanctonbury Ring*, by Bishop Stockwood.

The remaining quotations are from private teachings given to me through a number of sensitives.

I would also express great appreciation to Mrs Brenda Marshall, President of the College of Psychic Studies, and to Keith Ellis of Pilgrim Books, for valuable criticisms of the original text, and to Barbara and John Harland for infinite patience in deciphering and typing various versions of the manuscript.

CHAPTER ONE

A CHOICE OF HORIZON

1

IN EVERY man and woman there resides acknowledged or hidden a homesickness of the soul.

Many seek to project this homesickness outside themselves; upon a God in whom they hope they will some day safely rest; or upon a set of religious beliefs which offer an immediate guarantee through revelation; or upon a person of the opposite sex whose love they are sure will supply all they have not found in themselves. Or upon some cause, patriotic or political, whose success they are convinced will change the world and change men with it. Yet those who have achieved the most – the saints and the great artists – come to accept most fully and deeply the burden of human incompleteness in the most practical possible way, by overcoming it in themselves.

Over the last hundred years or so there has gradually come about a quiet invasion which in ways often thought impossible offers factual evidence of personal continuation into a much extended span beyond death. More important, it offers an opportunity for a growth of consciousness whilst here on earth and a deep and unexpected companionship. There is a great deal to suggest that this invasion has been initiated from another

source, from a thither world after death. It is not surprising that it has often been derided or disregarded.

This area of communication is a three-tiered one. The first tier as would be expected is an endeavour on many fronts to provide sometimes simple and sometimes very sophisticated evidence that men do survive their deaths. This evidence has been discussed in many books. The second tier lies in attempting to describe to us something of the *quality* of life as it is lived after death and the changes which in time this gradually brings about.

The third and most important tier offers the opportunity for companionship and fellowship to those on earth. This book attempts to describe and evaluate something of this adventure.

The first two are introductory; when all three are brought together they disclose an underlying plan, still in course of development. The first two tiers in fact require the third to give them full meaning. The fellowship involves a deeply based effort to help men to improve the quality of their life on earth, and in particular to get to know more now of their true selves, the hidden man or woman within, so that after death they will not find they are a stranger to themselves. Life here and life there are shown to be related and deeply reciprocal.

Clearly it is necessary to evaluate the stature of the communicators and why they should be believed when they earnestly declare that the values they have now found can gradually change and enrich us on earth in the same way as they themselves have come to be changed after death. They describe a process of learning by earning. They declare emphatically that an overall plan exists which has empowered them to help us, as they in turn are helped by senior beings further along the path of human achievement. What is offered is a human brotherhood, stretching out to touch our hidden inner

being in a close and intimate way. If clear evidence can be found that some of these communicators surpass our own present stature it implies that in time we also can grow to their height. Within our every day self awaits an inner self which responds to these values. It is this inner self which feels the homesickness.

2

Man bears within him a phoenix of his own, one most certainly not made of flesh and bones, but a self, partly familiar, partly strange, which arises to fly off after death and renew itself elsewhere. Many cannot imagine such a transition and conclude it to be as legendary as the phoenix itself. Yet – and this is indeed the point – the phoenix cannot fly off if it does not already exist now. The phoenix is the inner self which in earth experience can give proof of its reality. It is the link of continuity between man now and man hereafter. The phoenix contains man's superior part, slumbering or partly active.

The philosophy of living which is implied offers no universal panacea, nor of itself can it cause our earthly sense of incompleteness to disappear. The import of the communications is that we are engaged upon a strenuous working journey, which can bring about the gradual transformation of the inner consciousness of each. Such changes do not result through the intellectual adoption of a new set of ideas, but by living them out. It is pointed out that this is a very long and exacting task, in no way complete by the time death comes, but lasting far beyond one earth life, and that the prize has always to be paid for individually.

The purpose of psychical research has always been to examine what it is possible to measure by rigorous scientific methods. The psychical researcher of today is a specialist and the tools he uses impose disciplines upon his attention and, more important, limitations.

As with other areas of science, in much medical research for instance, what is looked for is what can be measured when the subjectivity of the patient or the recipient or the psychical researcher has been successfully eliminated by the techniques created – by double-blind tests, by statistics, by sophisticated laboratory randomising devices and the like. But what if the area of subjectivity itself offers valuable information which these methods purposefully and carefully exclude?

John Polkinghorne, F.R.S., writing in a wider context describes the situation precisely:

> Science derives its power from the experimental method; its ability to manipulate and interrogate the objects of its investigation. There are many other realms of experience, those characterised as personal rather than impersonal, where we do not have that manipulative power. . . . There is a wide range of human concern which involves commitment rather than detachment. Between science and religion at opposite ends of a spectrum there lie our experiences of beauty and of moral obligation. Our view of the world must do justice to that richness and complexity. . . . Science has many valuable truths to tell but it has achieved its success by restricting itself to a certain type of enquiry. There are other questions, of meaning and purpose, which can also validly be put.[1]

Thus, largely outside the present attention of the Society for Psychical Research, there exists a further body of material which as all can see does not fall within

scientific parameters. This material is partly of a personal nature and partly in the form of spiritual advice and teaching. For some, this exists at the heart of the subject.

The psychical field often seems so baffling and so confusing because much in it is relevant to one of these approaches, but not to the other. Hence those concerned are often not looking at the same thing, and look askance at one anothers' findings. So important parts of its material, though they often come welded together in mediumistic sources, are treated as two separated areas. Some parts are examined objectively, but the other part requires subjective exposure and assessment. It should not be overlooked that this other part occupies those areas which appear to be of most interest and concern to soi-distant communicators.

In commitment, a subjective element is of the essence. Commitment can well be slow, and usually will be all the better for that. Instant commitment is of little value without a subsequent discipline of careful testing by experience. Preliminary commitment can perfectly properly be provisional, can be little more than a willingness of attention through as many human faculties as a person can find within his resources. But this willingness is essential. In terms of the field of feeling, provisional commitment is not so very different after all from what a working hypothesis is in the intellectual field. If not subsequently justified, a provisional commitment can be withdrawn just as working hypotheses have frequently been discarded, though in the case of commitment, at rather more cost.

4

Serious communicators try to convey to us their present understanding of human verities. They wish us to explore

them. Active help from behind the scenes may be present in our private lives more often and more intimately than supposed. If so, tests of its reality must needs have a considerable area of subjectivity. Techniques of measure become replaced by a verdict gradually reached by use of the material in each person's own life situation.

Research will say, reasonably enough, that it must be left to choose the techniques it sees as best directed towards its aims. But if strict research leaves out a central part of the field, then a duty to examine it needs to be accepted by others who are not researchers, but are using other parts of their make-up in their search for truth.

A medium has a sensitivity to an area of perception which a researcher normally cannot himself reach; so he calls upon himself to be particularly alert to detect whether the information does not have the source claimed for it. He often expects this to be the case. Mediums find it hard to describe convincingly how mediumship works, but they do know how to become attuned to the areas within them where it functions. Researchers seldom can; this naturally produces extra doubt in them. Nevertheless, if the mediumistic faculty speaks truly at times, something however elusive in man's own nature should be able to recognise it as valid. It would be strange if it did not. It is an important fact that paranormal events are seen to be by no means limited to working mediums; they sometimes come about in spontaneous ways, as many independent veridical experiences have shown. Powers of reception are more intimate and more widespread than often assumed. For many people they are hard to accept when they go against daily commonsense, or are sometimes seemingly very unlikely. Yet in exploring mediumistic sensitivity it begins to appear that we are exploring a faculty latent within human nature in general, and not just an unusual one found in a few. True mediumship implies

a *deepening* of receptivity which enables a transfer of material, from the level at which it is perceived, to the everyday level where it is not. It forms a bridge of consciousness for the aid of those who cannot cross it for themselves.

5

Leaving aside dramatic spontaneous events a large number of persons show that they possess in simple ways something of what is best called the psi factor. In a quiet manner it is very often present behind ordinary civilised behaviour.

A hostess, considering her guests, often senses their feeling-tones towards her and each other and also within themselves, and seeks to bring the overall atmosphere of her party into harmony; she is then working near to the edge of psi perception. What is sensed though unspoken is part of the feeling-texture with which her hospitality deals. This forms for her an enjoyable interior skill.

Like any other human faculties psi can be developed into well or ill regulated disciplines. A hostess for instance who temporarily permits herself to use her insights for personal spite or malicious curiosity can sharply diminish her contribution instead of enhancing it.

Psi deals with living human processes, of which the nuts and bolts of a situation are only the outer shell. It lives in a world of values, sometimes moves in deep waters, and is drenched in qualitative feelings. Hence psi perceptions can be reassuring, uncomfortable, supportive, penetrating, challenging and sometimes insightful and creative.

Not long after his death a former minister of religion defined it thus:

> The psi factor is the sparking plug of the creative impulse in life . . . It is behind and contained in every original breakthrough of the thinkers, scientists, philosophers, theologians, musicians and artists. It is the essence of original and new creation on all levels. Just as materialism pervades and invades all departments of your life on earth today, so here you cannot fail to be influenced – on some levels perhaps superficially – by the pervading and over-riding dominance of moral values and surety of faith in the intrinsic goodness of a sacramental universe.[2]

If the psi factor works widely in this way, then the professional psychic is only making a specialised use of an intrinsic human quality.

In the meaningful inner world of psi the boundaries of the self are not so sharply drawn as in the outer world. The hostess for instance may become aware of more than the guest wishes her to know about himself and perhaps the guest uses a similar privilege towards the hostess. This is an important characteristic, and becomes well understood, as the world of inner sensing becomes familiar.

Discarnate communications state over and over that the surviving part of man is this inner self, operating much more freely than before because now without the clogging constraints of the physical body. This inner self at times, by help of the psi factor, already draws from the further world instruction which can slowly well up into the mind and feelings of everyday. The inner self is able to endorse this because it already knows more in some ways than does the outer man. Considered as a fact, at first this may be somewhat difficult to accept. Yet the more closely its working is studied, the more natural this becomes. Discarnate teachers bring a better balance between these two parts of man's being. But it is as important to them as to us that men and women, however inwardly developed,

should also continue to keep their feet firmly on the ground.

The hope is that the inner man will listen to the full message intended; the deeper discarnate purpose is not primarily to prove a continuing existence. External evidence is sometimes a necessary end in itself, but more often its purpose is to help awaken, or re-awaken the inner man who somewhere in his own being already knows something of the inferences which evidence imparts. Fuller communication by its very nature best links itself with the larger inner man. Then like is speaking to like. We pass then beyond the intimations of the hostess to a deeper level of the self.

Clearly it is of utmost importance whether or not this sense that we are somehow more than our present selves is indeed a true voice of a part of self which, on surviving death, will gradually come to know its wholeness; a future inheritance speaking to us now, in however inarticulate a way.

6

It is easy to denigrate the early messages of survival from new arrivals, accompanied sometimes by simplistic assumptions which those who send them usually abandon later after further experience. They are not intended to be examined too closely and are for those neither qualified nor wishful to be qualified at sophisticated intellectual levels. Since people exist in the inner world at many levels just as on earth, there can be corresponding messages to suit.

So allowance has to be made that what is appropriate to one level of spiritual understanding is not so to another. The teacher's material is not to be judged by the tales for

spiritual children which many listeners first hear but by very adult conceptions which can follow later.

One seeks legal or medical advice because one is out of one's depth in such fields. Superior expertise is sought. In seeking advice from spiritual guides in what is at first so seemingly strange a relationship, it is natural to feel wary. A spiritual guide cannot exhibit any brass plate or diploma to guarantee his competence.

Such a guide therefore faces two grave handicaps. His credentials must emerge largely from the teaching he gives, and this teaching is inevitably misaligned to some degree by the mind of the sensitive through whom he speaks, and also – though this is not so evident – by the listener too.

How can this be overcome? As in many other situations its value only emerges gradually through experiment and experience. Some risk and adventure have to be accepted. Then an outstandingly happy and fruitful partnership can be reached. Obviously at first the student on earth brings his own armoury of judgment to bear. He will ask himself in a number of ways what the guide has to offer, and why he has approached the student. Is the guide both honest and wise? Is he truly aware of the pupil's inner problems and needs? Is his help caring? Is it precise, or no more than vague, soft, uplift?

The necessary requirement in the pupil is that he does not reject the situation outright, but is willing to take serious part in the experiment. Whether he wishes it or not, his own integrity is at much at stake as that of the guide. He needs to play fair. But different people quite rightly need very varying degrees of experience before coming to their verdict.

Both we and our communicators, the testimony declares, live within a graded continuum of consciousness. The continuum is an important concept. It implies

steps on a spiritual Jacob's Ladder; each step provides, and at the same time limits, its own degree of vision. The depths of the continuum can only gradually be won. New areas are at first sensed only at the borders of one's present sensibility; further evidence of their reality comes by whole hearted action upon what has been so far understood.

What is claimed as spoken from discarnate sources, however diluted, needs to exhibit coherence with other spiritual paths and to resonate with them. If all men and women belong to a continuum, they can be expected ultimately to resonate with one another within it, even though imperfectly, and not necessarily in a way instantly apparent. Delving may be needed. Theological exclusiveness is not helpful here.

What communicators offer is not in the least in the theological sense revelation, nor dependent upon it. They seek to present what is relevant to one's spiritual present, and to offer a way of working towards one's spiritual future; they endeavour to extend the present horizon.

When these communicators speak of a continuum, it is always implied that this remains both beyond our full comprehension, and theirs also.

To quote a recent communication claimed to be from Conan Doyle:

> What the end is we cannot tell you. No one that I've met can tell me. There are worlds beyond worlds, and I use this term more in a spiritual sense than a geographical sense . . . no one really can tell you because to us it is the unsolvable question.

In all this field we cannot dogmatise (or rather we can, but it is a great obstacle to truth to do so) for to dogmatise imposes limits just where the mind needs to open itself more, sometimes perhaps in a seemingly childlike way.

There is after all, the best of all precedents to make ourselves as little children.

In the earthly areas of the continuum we are already in one of many mansions of the Gospel; not always in the same one as the earth companions next to us but the one to which our present stature gives access. It is part of the truth as seen from one part of the road; our present step upon the Jacob's Ladder. In turn all teachers, here and beyond, cannot be expected to come from the same mansion. They bring differing fruits from the general harvest. Yet it is not too hard to recognise when quality of experience surpasses our own. Quality here, as in all else, conveys itself. It also provides an unspoken comment upon our own quality.

> We want man to find himself at his own level. Each his own saviour. The stretching hand and the response from our world – but only so far as he stretches his hand can we respond.[3]

Sources of Quotations

1   *The Times* 18th February 1984
2   Rev. G. S. Whitby (posthumous)
3   A private teaching

CHAPTER TWO

THE COMING OF THE TEACHER

1

NOT SURPRISINGLY, the first reaction of most people towards a discarnate teacher is that they have no need of him. They prefer to manage their life for themselves. What then has such a teacher to offer which cannot be obtained from earthly teachers or learned direct from life? The first answer to such an over-broad question is: 'Nothing'. In essence the whole task of such a teacher is to be true towards the wisdom of the ages and towards the processes which life itself brings about.

His purpose is to help gradually to bring about on earth the same ways of learning as are in use in the further world, and which all of us will encounter there in due course. These ways are by a mutual interpenetratation of thought, by demonstration through experience, by the gradual deepening of perception, and above all through living in an ever-fuller companionship of love.

Such a purpose can very naturally be misunderstood. It is not to give his students an easy path into happier realms after death, nor is it to shelter them from the hardships and endurances of earth. It is to help them achieve maximum spiritual growth and fulfilment of purpose. A guide's working tools are his love and

wisdom, humour, compassion, and a deep insight into human character.

> Too often we see those who feel drawn into the spirit disregard everything appertaining to the material; this is not right, it is not necessary. Whilst people are encased in their flesh we can still train them in their mind and spirit because the mind-spirit relationship is very near.[1]

It is part of the teaching's strength and not a weakness that it lies within the broad stream of human experience. Nevertheless discarnate teaching does offer a unique contribution because it also relates to a field of living of which much of mankind prefers to remain unaware, or to largely ignore. Further, and very important, it is presented in terms which relate very precisely to each pupil. The guide draws very close to his charge because his insight needs to be directed to his special and immediate situation. The pupil finds the teacher does not abandon his task lightly. It is a serious relationship or it is nothing.

It is not surprising that such a relationship – deeply traditional though it is in some ways – is to most modern people unfamiliar, unexpected and perhaps unwelcome. The teacher has to make use of two difficult routes, by making use of the services of a medium or sensitive, and, usually later, by direct telepathic contact with the more interior aspects of the pupil's mind. The pupil's independence however is always insisted upon.

> The important thing is that I want you to be free. I want your thinking to be free. I want you to be so free that what we have been talking to you about will bear your critical analysis and will still ring through to you as truth and acceptable.[2]

The teaching is thus concerned with each pupil's own spiritual commitment or possible commitment. Quite

THE COMING OF THE TEACHER

rightly the pupil does not give this lightly. In any teaching situation the collaboration of the pupil is obviously vital. To the newcomer the obvious question is likely to be: why should I pay any attention to what these alleged teachers say?

This is a robust enough attitude. The guides' way of dealing with objections is very practical. They neither claim nor protest too much. Their method of answering is the very simple one of producing year in and year out the goods they see are necessary to their listener. In spiritual things as in others the proof of the pudding lies in the eating. Those who only glance at the pudding will not know as much about it as those who taste it. It is perfectly reasonable for some people to say that neither the look of the pudding, nor the kitchen which produced it, inspire any confidence to taste it. No one can object to such a stance.

These teachers as will be seen later in no way ask or wish to be taken on trust. They are pleased when a pupil brings to the encounter important parts of his nature by which to judge the material. They do not ask that he shall bring the whole of himself, for, as the pupil will find, it is not at all likely that he has yet succeeded in finding it. For that reason he cannot bring it. One of the teacher's tasks is to help him find it, or some of it.

> We are trying to take fear away from the people of the world, we are trying to heighten their perceptions, and take them into the inner core of being. You know the simile of an onion: we take a skin away, and another skin away. This is what we try to do with people, take the skins away.[3]

2

The validity of communication as genuine experience grows if a sizeable number of people from various walks

of life find themselves accepting it, within the different values of their separate temperaments. They provide a concourse of valuations, based on independent life experiences. Before communication with a guide is accepted as valid, a considerable period of scepticism is normal.

The guide after all cannot be seen in his own person: he is obliged to make some use of part of the medium's personality. In almost every case he will be someone unknown, whom the listener has never met. His memory therefore has nothing with which to compare the teacher's presentation of himself. The teacher has to make his impact completely *de novo* establishing his reality by whether his values lodge themselves in his listener, and awake a living resonance there. The listener will also be judging from more everyday levels how far his presence rings true as a human being. Whatever his views express, they will be expected to be reasonably consistent, clear enough to permit of accurate understanding, and gradually commanding respect. In time, if the communicator passes these tests, and is accepted as a teacher, he will be expected to provide a wider horizon – intellectually and spiritually – than the recipient's own. This will be what makes him worth listening to.

This is naturally well understood by the guide. He claims no authority either of person or of office. The teachings of The Tibetan telepathically received by Alice Bailey, all contain the same foreword:

> . . . I am a brother of yours, who has travelled a little longer upon the Path than has the average student, and has therefore incurred greater responsibilities.
>
> The books are sent out with no claim for their acceptance. They may, or may not, be correct, true and useful. It is for you to ascertain their truth by right practice and by the exercise of the intuition . . .

16

If the statements meet with eventual corroboration, or are deemed true under the test of the Law of Correspondences, then that is well and good. But should this not be so, let not the student accept what is said.[4]

In slightly more personal terms the teacher who adopted the name Silver Birch says:

I am not an infallible spirit teacher who never makes mistakes and has achieved the summit of progress. That cannot be so . . . because the more you achieve the more you realise there is to be achieved . . .

We never ask you to take us on trust. We do not say that you must do what we suggest. Nor do we insist that there are no other ways by which you can obtain a greater attunement with the Great Spirit.

What we do affirm, and with all the strength at our command, is that the truths of the spirit can be tested by your reason, intelligence and experience. There is no threat of punishment if you say we have told you things which you do not accept . . .

If anything we say from our life cannot pass the bar of your reason and makes it revolt, if it insults your intelligence, reject it.

We have to appeal not to the lowest, but to the highest within you, so that you will give your co-operation and allegiance because you desire to do so.[5]

This attitude is absolutely basic to all this school of teaching. Its material is derived from two areas: gained from former experience on earth, and earned in an enriching way in the different environment after death. To receive acceptance today this will have to be much more than wish-fulfilment, or a rehash of religious orthodoxy. Listeners will seek to know how much of their own character will prove of value when carried over after death and ask what processes in this further life will bring them new insight. They will assess whether the teacher's

words are truly drawn from deeper and different experience than their own.

Confidence, naturally enough, grows if one finds that a teacher first offers a convincing insight into one's own earth character and its accompanying problems. He shows he can help the pupil to loosen the knots in his character by offering an altered perspective on his problems. When the pupil comes to see them in a new way, the problems often largely disappear as a result. The teacher is expected too to speak to the listener's own interior world with more effective insight than the listener has been able to acquire for himself. Clearly this involves a matter of stature.

If a student schools himself to come to the teacher openly, without too tight a schedule of preconceived tests, demands and concepts, he will have discovered one of the open secrets; that the teacher needs living-space to allow him to present both himself and his material in his own way. Only thus can a wider framework be presented.

A gradual but true collaboration can then begin. On both sides, as with more ordinary relationships, patience and continuing good will are part of the ballast which help to keep the ship moving forward steadily.

3

The guide offers us a goal of *being*. In doing so he brings his own quality of peace. He tells us we can already take some of the same steps as he; earth life is as open to these as is the life he now enjoys. Hence the learning process he shares with us. In fact, as he emphasises, all learning is *continuous* learning.

It does not end at a fixed point of achievement and certainly not comparatively soon after the event of death.

Many expect a judgment already finalised through the choices and happenings of the life just concluded, a retrospective judgment with rewards and punishments on a foreordained scale. Teachers declare on the contrary that the process of judgment is really one of self-judgment, or more accurately self-recognition. It shows us what we have really made ourselves to be, and the consequences which flow therefrom. These continue until we ourselves set about altering or modifying them. As we act, we learn.

4

What needs to be learned may prove surprising to the present view we take of ourselves. To take a simple and obvious illustration. Let us suppose one has cheated a considerable number of people, even if at the time one gave oneself the most logical and convincing reasons that it was not really cheating, nor, properly regarded, even wrong – thus cheating oneself as well. To meet again every one of those who have been cheated cannot but be an unpleasant confrontation in which one is shown up, for the true facts are now clearly seen by all. However long delayed, this involves remorse for former actions, and then the need for some kind of restitution. The burden has been lifted from the formerly oppressed to the oppressor. As a result of this the oppressor learns, in time, to change his own nature. In this way, although the consequences have been inescapable, he too ultimately draws a benefit from them. But the benefit has a price, that of gradual and painful recognition of his own self. No external wrath has been imposed by any external God. He is cleansed by the later consequences of his own former actions.

> There has been no punishment meted out and justice in the other world is justice such as man never knows on earth.[6]

Here at work is one of the basic spiritual laws which as guides teach, underly life. A law of compensation, of equilibrium and balance.

Why, it will be asked, does this continuation of life result in the *moral* consequences described? Why should not the further span continue to repeat the apparent escapes from consequences so familiar on earth? Why should not the race continue to the strong? But all the discarnate testimony clearly points to the contrary. It shows that many of these burdens of mortality – one's mental and emotional attitudes – at first accompany one into the inner world. There they await regeneration. They do not disappear of themselves. Moreover it is found to be impossible to live fully in the larger inner world whilst still clinging on to familiar but now outmoded things of the former outer self.

Consequences, however, are only part of the story. There is as well growth and development, and here the testimony is emphatic. The better parts of man are as fully engaged as his worst. Provender is for both.

Teachers are therefore needed. The inner side of life on earth and the inner world beyond clearly provide very deep areas of relationship. Communication can be through words, but later more truly through a mutual and free-flowing process of telepathy. Telepathy is speech grown clearer. It is hard to share in experience not yet one's own, but communicators are most anxious to help us to do so; to show us a way to come to understand something of that experience, to deepen spiritual insight and thus come to it for ourselves. This is a difficult task for both sides.

> It is a very strange and complex pattern that you people on the earth are part of, how we can utilise one person to

transmit to another things or words or books – this is part of our way of working through others, how we get the individual woven into a fabric, so that they all become part of sharing the whole. We must make a supreme effort to quicken and deepen the earth people's consciousness to make them again lift themselves, to make themselves more attuned so that they might receive intuitively without the voice of the medium.[7]

This suggests that they know us better than we know ourselves. They look for the hidden self, more valuable than the daily self which weighs it down.

But men and women unfortunately often shut away or fail to find their own potentially valuable qualities which therefore remain for the time being largely unexpressed. That can form a tragedy. Guides are able to help because they usually possess, and demonstrate as well developed within themselves the qualities unawakened or banished in the one they aim to help. Should this not enable them to see more and to have more to give? By their own consciousness, playing upon lacking parts in the man on earth, they impregnate him with their own qualities, but of course it is only the man on earth who can bring about the parturition.

5

After death we continue where we left off, but with the privilege of self-judgment growing more and more clear as part of our change of condition. Some may think this is almost too simple to be true. However, if true it cannot be doubted that it is logical. It is also reassuring if consequences are not unalterable but can gradually be overcome. We can remake our role in the life ahead by remaking ourselves. That is the important thing. We can

also do it on earth. The teacher is speaking to our present as well as to our future. The scenes around us, found after death, will be wide or narrow according to the dimensions of our own nature. What we are able to see depends upon what we are, upon our moral cognition and inseparable from it. The same process, though a little more hidden, can be observed at work on earth. Teachers concern themselves much with this. In doing so they are teaching simultaneously how best to live both on earth and beyond it.

6

Instruction is naturally graded to what a pupil can absorb.

When the guide speaks to the everyday outer man, he is not of course addressing the whole of him. How can he? Therefore much early work lies in bringing confidence to the pupil to begin to live more deeply than through the comfortable habits of his daily self. The guide often delegates this early work to relatives and peers who demonstrate that since their death they have gradually enlarged *their* horizons. They try to tell a little of what they now see and which has altered them as a result. Their continuing existence guarantees his own. It is very usual for the guide to defer his appearance. If the pupil listens to his former peers with care, then the guide will come and give him instructions. He seeks to speed up spiritual living on earth, through a quickening in the individual.

Just because relatives and peers are closer to the pupil's outer self, they are still somewhat bound up, as he is, with personal and local concerns. Their advice, though good, lies within a limited sphere. However much they do indeed give in generous support and help, they are likely to be tolerant towards some degree of self-interest

because they themselves have not altogether left it behind. Inevitably in time the pupil finds himself beginning to look beyond their help. Sometimes he hardly knows why. Really the new horizon is beckoning him on earth in exactly the same way as it is beckoning to the relatives and peers beyond. Things do not stand still for either.

7

A guide's work is necessarily rather uphill though he does not reveal it is so. Everyday facets of the pupil are often reluctant and resistant. The guide has to win these over, has to convince the pupil that he is on his side, and that he knows what he is talking about. Perhaps the pupil believes himself willing to listen. So he may be, but has he the equipment within him needed to respond fully? If not the guide has to awaken it.

Naturally if the outer and the inner are not in harmony the teacher will meet with conflict in the relationship. After all nearly every man and woman on earth is his or her own private walking predicament, though certainly without fully knowing it. This predicament consists in not recognising much in one's own nature, which, from behind the scenes, governs the flaws of character and temperament and forms their true sources however plausibly they can be attributed elsewhere.

> You have to remember that you are imperfect beings living in an imperfect world. If the Great Spirit wanted you to be perfect you would not have been placed on earth. You have the choice, the free will, as to how you utilise the gifts, the powers, the talents with which you are endowed.
>
> The essence of life on earth is it offers stark contrasts and polarities. It provides goodness and the lack of goodness . . .

> The object of earthly life is to make available a variety of experiences, to enable the soul to exercise its divine potential and emerge stronger as a result. And so you will have crime, sin and violence.[8]

In coming to recognise these imperfect aspects and to cleanse them, the inner part of the self gradually takes more command. The focus of living gradually changes. All this lies very much in the guide's attention. He cares about it more than the pupil at first is able to do. The pupil's outer self, broadly speaking, is insufficiently concerned with the guide's work on his very behalf, therefore the approach of the guide needs at times to be indirect and subtle. Gradually the pupil comes to recognise this, and begins to look out for apparently irrelevant sentences which are really inner instruction. These are often the more meaningful because they have to be thus introduced with a certain element of sleight-of-hand. It is a way of bypassing outer resistances much as the Freudian dream does. In order to pick them up correctly the pupil has to be alert. The guide of course is aware of the degree of his pupil's interior resources; he carefully studies it, as the pupil finds out.

It becomes apparent that the guide-pupil relationship has a degree of likeness to other teaching relationships of an inner type, where for instance the drama takes place in the novitiate or the monastery. In both, the unworthy parts of the pupil are the target for change, re-alignment and ultimate transformation. The difference when a guide is the teacher is that the pupil remains out in the world, free to accept or reject, not bound by any vows or imposed disciplines. Relationships with a guide whilst seemingly of apparent ease, are nevertheless a modern equivalent for earlier more formal and harsher disciplines.

8

As the student comes under closer attention his outer and inner sides become less opposed, and begin to fall into more fruitful counterpoint. After all they have to live together within the same person. In place of mediaeval monastic disciplines undergone in order to devalue the outer self altogether – as it were to cast it out like an orphan – the modern purpose lies more in a gradual change of emphasis. Some of the outer values, at first so insistent, and with their growing and complicating demands, fall away quite naturally once the pupil recognises he is free to ignore their insistences; free too to grow tired of them. In the supreme example of Mother Teresa, every moment of outer life is devoted and dedicated to an inner purpose of love which, because all distractions have steadily been put aside, has become simplicity itself. A guide does not demand such lofty (and to most of us frightening) aims for his student. He respects his present possible pace. The student comes to see he has been planted where he is on earth firmly and benevolently by life's laws, and that he is constantly making choices which, however slightly, are altering and re-creating his own being. These are the areas upon which the guide's kindly insights are focussed.

9

Of course it is an essential part of one's passport to earth that one has faults. Many, whilst admitting to a few faults, feel these can fairly easily be reduced or brushed off altogether when wished, and that on the whole they do not matter too much. The faults one is aware of, a guide has said, are the superficial ones; real work only starts by

becoming sensitive to undiscovered ones. They are not to be found by easy observation. By working to put right recognised faults the layers of more serious ones begin to be revealed.

Acting to transform faults however must never be in order to obtain a supposed increased reward but simply because they *are* faults and therefore a blot upon the moral landscape of the world just as much as an ugly building in a physical landscape. That is hard fact.

Adapting the old saying, it is of no use the workman blaming his tools when the tools are made up of his own character. Since a much-extended life lies ahead the pace can be restful if so preferred, instead of one of haste and panic, during the process of transforming the ball and chain upon one's feet into positive qualities. The pupil recognises too that the guide never blames him; he simply gives encouragement. Inevitable imperfection is the very warp upon which earth experience has to be threaded. The guide is always generous in recognising where the imperfect pattern also has good strands.

In human relationships much complaint and ill-will grows from disappointed expectations. This melts away when insight heals the bruises which lie behind the disappointments. Petty domestic wars can often be terminated readily. If the warfare is not real enough to have a long term continuation, why not end it swiftly? If however there can be no mending, the breaking up of a relationship, however painful, can be a treaty which, unlike some treaties, can end a war for good. Small issues, in the light of long term, are no longer the former monstrous giants they seemed; the false life which has sustained them evaporates easily enough. Time as we say is a great healer; the certainty of extended time a much greater one. The pupil has often obscured things by

looking at them through the lens of his outer nature; he
need no longer altogether do so.

It is a natural thing for man to want to be happy, and it has
taken us many lives to find that happiness comes from within,
and is met with happiness from without, but unless the
happiness is stretched out from within, and the peace comes
from within, you cannot receive, you are as a block of ice.
This is what is happening in the world where men are
building up a hard casing about themselves, sensitive, kind
people whom life has hurt, who have felt their ideals rejected
and discarded, who feel that they have not succeeded. They
build up this hard veneer, not understanding that it is based
on man's own values of what is success.[9]

10

But how can we tell whether the guide is right, or if his
words only offer delusion, or are even intended ultimately
to deceive? It is not wise at all to take the bona fides of
every guide for granted. Is his very facelessness used to
hide his true motive? There is a very good key to tell a
guide's status. No true one will claim too much for himself
or his pupil or make over-forceful demands; his
clavichord is well-tempered.

'Suppose it all to be wrong?' is the question bound at
times to trouble both medium and listener. Unlike
orthodox religion, the teacher does not seek to overcome
the doubt by assurance of revelation. He simply says
'Look more deeply into your self, and you will find your
own assurance there'.

Thus by the very training he gives, a true guide is
providing the tools of discrimination which will in time
enable the pupil to recognise his own stature a little more
truly. Right use of his experiences both on earth and

beyond has enabled the guide to purify himself, and this he explains is just what his pupil can do. The laws may be somewhat densely hidden on earth; nevertheless they are at work. By inner development we gradually come to see this. So in time we become in ourselves the confirmation of the guide's teaching. Our own natures prove his point. Is it so strange, fellow human being as he is, that his later experience and our present experience run in parallel and that the same true values exist and go on existing for both? On death a man remains still in the same boat; he does not transfer to quite a different boat, headed in some different direction.

A well-known posthumous contribution from Oliver Lodge puts it in this way:

> These two bodies are his here and now . . . the clay to the potter . . . It is worth while endeavouring to take not only himself, as he calls this limited physical body, in hand but to take his two selves . . . and perfect them so that he has a second body, his spirit body, ready perfect . . . when the time of death comes.[10]

Dean Matthews of St Paul's made a somewhat similar statement in his lifetime:

> . . . it seems to me reasonable to believe that we are now weaving our spiritual bodies as we go along. They are being formed by our thoughts and acts of will and imagination during this life.

It can readily be seen why the guide has little interest in distracting questions of what one should or should not do. Whether for good, or comfort, or even for base self-advantage, the pupil's decision has to be his own. He cannot call upon the guide (though he often tries to) to short-circuit his task. In brute fact, whether his decision is right or wrong, he can learn from it. Different decisions bring about different lessons; that is all, and some

unfortunately are more costly than others, especially if they directly involve other people.

Spiritual levels gradually change. Each student seeks the values which speak to his present condition, and at the same time puts out antennae towards more exacting values. The guide calls on one's ability to commence to hit more difficult targets.

Life which has passed is no vanished blank period, gone for nothing. Many men and women become ready to absorb deeper teaching as a result of former lessons imposed by life itself, through disciplines which at the time were sometimes difficult to face, but which now bear fruit. The rich complexity and apparent confusions of earth life lead in many different ways from one step on the Jacob's Ladder to the next. Why seek to herd others into the same particular and possibly narrow pathway one has known for oneself? Every level, sincerely explored, offers its own opportunities for commitment. Teaching is available up and down the scale.

There is no sense in longer life extended over thousands of years, without this growth to accompany it. Else life would be as painful a trial as to the Wandering Jew.

Let us now look at some of the sustaining values which the guide offers to us, from himself, for our own direct use.

Sources of Quotations

1   A private teaching
2   id.
3   id.
4   Alice A. Bailey books: A statement by The Tibetan

5 *Light from Silver Birch*, p. 203
6 A private teaching
7 id.
8 *Light from Silver Birch*, p. 19
9 A private teaching
10 *Journal* of the Society for Psychical Research, June 1945

CHAPTER THREE

CONTINUOUS LEARNING

1

A CHILD SENT to a kindergarten is given the simple things it can so far absorb. In terms of new environment, an adult after death is sometimes still a child in understanding. (So, as a guide once drily remarked, are many seventy-year-olds on earth). There are many grades to pass through after death. All need instructors.

> It is no mystery. It is a perfect plan, that you return to God in your way, with guidance.[1]

Teaching and learning in the thither world beyond death therefore has many levels. It is lengthy because of the transforming energy it requires of pupils. People learn as the result of changing themselves. In order to change, they need to see themselves a little more clearly. We find when old friends return to communicate that they often make a confession of former mistakes. What they say is sometimes very touching. For instance an intellectual who had formerly rather looked down upon his wife, confessed how he now found that, after all, her spiritual stature had exceeded his. It was she who had made the sacrifices within the marriage. Evidently it helps to express in this way what have later come to be seen as errors of character.

The worlds before and after death are related by a common spiritual order. This principle parallels the one made by the scientist that the natural laws he is studying will be found to be orderly. To examine seriously whatever experiences those in the thither world are attempting to impart, requires the same fundamental premise of a world of order.

It then makes sense that surrounding and permeating earthly life, a fuller universe exists however little we as yet know of it. It would be hard to think of planet earth existing without the galaxy in which it moves. So too with one's own spark of life. The individual can be existing in a far larger and more purposeful world than he can as yet encompass. Teachers in the thither world attempt to demonstrate something of this to us.

After all if man's span exceeds his present days on earth, his make-up and his destiny alike must surely be more complex than if devised for a single span. Some of his real nature may meanwhile be obscured by the limited focus of earth living. There are likely to be matters of consequence waiting to be imparted after death, and as far as our limited insights permit on earth too.

An important task of the guide is therefore to awaken man to his own true earth potential. The student is invited to find in himself an increased capacity for the opening, or further opening, of his inner mind. Men and women are asked to look for parts of their own being where they have not yet functioned and to become much more familiar with them. At first conflict and lack of alignment is likely to arise between long-established intellectual patterns and these delicate and sometimes intuitive perceptions.

You know words are very poor things to express what belongs to a celestial whole . . . and to the experience of being in tune with a God law, a cosmic law. This is all

important; it is not magic, it is not something beyond anyone's reach, but it involves great discipline; meditation and a great deal of search for meaning and truth.[2]

We should never forget that we must always . . . claim what is ours; not to expect that it will gradually become assimilated without our asking for it. The aspiration is one of the great factors. And this is one of our big difficulties with your earth that not sufficient of the earth's population have spiritual aspiration; they have a spiritual need but not a spiritual aspiration.[3]

The hidden spiritual forces behind the world are spoken of by the teacher in whatever terms he judges will best fructify the pupil's soul at the present. Thus he may speak of the Deity in Christian terms. Or he may speak of the Father-Mother God, or of the Architect of the Universe, or in terms of the God who is within and behind the Sun, or simply of a God-force. In time it is likely to come to matter little to the pupil which language is used. All indeed are ancient, and have inspired many men in distant pasts. The student is taught to be flexible, to look for the substance behind the name, to be willing to worship in any temple. He is asked to loosen orthodox conceptions when he sees they are in danger of becoming fetters. He is invited more fully into the brotherhood of man.

2

The tone of a guide's voice is one of experience. It is simple and direct. Similarly the morality offered, with its constantly unfolding layers, does not easily harden into a set code. Codes too readily come to insist on what can be basically no more than local irrelevance of behaviour.

What then does a guide offer in place of a code? He offers something very simple, the principle of *motive*.

Motive he says is what determines the value of acts. No teacher would condemn a penniless man who steals bread for his infants. He might of course ask how it was the man became penniless; was he helpless in a war-ravaged or parched country? Or was it his own lowering of behaviour which brought about the lacks? Motive can be simple, but it can also sharpen into depth and subtlety. After all how often is a man really aware of his motive, how often does he hide it from himself? Are there slants which he prefers to ignore? Does he deceive himself with obstinate convictions he will not shift? For whose benefit is he really working? Who pays the true cost of his actions? There is a familiar Spanish proverb: 'Do what you will, but then pay the price'. There can be great hidings-up of motives; sooner or later the price will include unveiling them. But no guide condemns failure. Failure, for him, is a valuable way to learn. What he does like is for the failed one to pick himself up and try again. And trying may involve a change of motive.

It will be said that the guide must lead us somewhere. What sort of guide is he if he leaves it all to us? Of course he does not leave it all to us, though he entirely respects free will. He indicates values, and lives them himself in his relationship with us.

Let us make a list of some qualities he appears to value most, but remembering that it remains an earthly list and not his.

The first fundamental distinction is that he praises qualities which unite and bring expansion. Other qualities will lead to contraction and separation. Says Goethe's Mephistopheles: 'I am the Spirit which denies'. Yet evil qualities, through the failures they can bring (often at first not recognized as such) can lead in a mysterious manner to an outcome for good. Transformation of consciousness is one of the miracles in human

nature which a guide is always working to help bring about.

The sets of qualities are, in their way, straightforward to the point of being obvious. It would be hard, after all, for them to be otherwise. Part of their value is that the long history of human striving largely supports them.

VIRTUES: Love, simplicity, harmlessness;
insight, tolerance, forgiveness;
patience, perseverance, generosity of spirit;
fortitude, courage;
inner sensitivity to those in this world and in the further world.

VICES: Greed, exploitation, cruelty;
condemnation and denial of other men's and women's values;
disobedience to nature;
defiance of law, persistence in evil;
false intellectual sophistication, dogma, insensitivity.

Behind simplicities lie complex tasks. The guide's insight seeks how those personal errors which call for regeneration first came about. What steps need to be retraced? What new steps won? How have virtues become foreshortened into apparently justified selfishness?

To look back into the gross errors which history records, is also to ask if the personal history of most of us is likely to be any more wise than the general performance of mankind.

Unless enough men and women work upon their own private regeneration – though to do it for self-interest would be deeply contradictory – is the regeneration of the world in the least likely to come about?

The fundamental purpose, as we have seen, is to help men and women to see themselves in their true setting, one wider than that of daily life, and to help them to live in fuller awareness of it. It is equally important to use this awareness to serve earth life more fully, and never to deny or hide from it. On earth much in the inner nature is often only dimly sensed, or missed altogether. Hence Matthew Arnold's divine discontent. Man is in an intermediary state. His own faults keep him there.

> It is so idle for people to talk about our world as a world where you receive punishment; there is no punishment as punishment is understood in your world, nobody stands in a dock, nobody has a judge or jury; we just are surrounded by those with greater light, who support us and strengthen us in our frailties as we look at what was amiss, or where we erred, but we are not left alone with it. We see where we hurt or where we neglected or omitted something that was not so much a duty but an obligation, and the golden group around just gives us support and strength to observe it. They are not left comfortless and alone but they are gradually being loved, each one that comes over, whatever cause, whatever evil man has condemned him for. How dare man condemn man, when he does not understand the other's soul and spirit?[4]

To acquire a degree of skill in utilising his inner qualities of character comes about when man learns to live more easily with his intuition. Of course as with any other human quality, intuition can be false, mistaken, impulsive, self-manipulating. The more deeply it penetrates, the greater the delicacy of conscience called for in its use. When listened to with humility, it has a quality of conveying its own truth in areas which lie beyond the middle registers of everyday use, and nearer to the homeland of the true spiritual self.

It is a common complaint, as man drags his earthly footsteps, that it is all very well for the guide to talk; it is easy to see him as living a life relieved from all our own difficulties and to accuse him of failing to understand our own problems. But the guide does know and remembers very well the difficulties of earth, and demonstrates that he does so. In fact the guide often establishes his reality by the very method of gradually revealing how well he understands the pupil, better indeed than the pupil himself does.

> Think along the line of all religion and no religion; there are no sinners in our world, there are those who are enlightened and those who are less enlightened. It is a question of degree. In your world there has to be punishment by man, it does not solve the problem, rather does it drive the hatred and the lack of adjustment deeper into that person.[5]

> Suffering brought about by cruelty, cruelty to oneself, cruelty to another; we ask you to look at it passionately and dispassionately, to *care* about something, to care about what is happening to people. No man can live on the mountain top detached from the world. You must become identified with it. You must care about it and pray that waves of love and light and understanding will roll on, penetrating to that difficulty, that self-destruction and turn it into good, redirect it from destruction to construction.[6]

His insight sees the seeds in the pupil's inner being which are awaiting nourishment. He values the pupil's inner self as far more real than his outer imprisoned self. His vision is upon the pupil's future. This, as a guide will freely admit, can occasionally be a cause of error on his part; with his speed of thought it is easy for him to expect the pupil to achieve sooner than he does. This can then appear as a prophecy gone wrong. The uncertain element lies in the pupil's free will.

In no way at all however is the guide an ineffectual idealist. His attention to practical things is realistic and often pithy.

Thus when a teacher was once asked what was the right form of words for the marriage ceremony, he replied: 'Of what use are the right words if the wrong people are marrying one another?' When a pupil defended shooting foxes because they stole his chickens, the guide asked how he thought the fox feels about human predators who constantly lock away *his* food. The guide added 'Suppose the fox has the gun'.

A guide certainly has ways of keeping the pupil's self-importance in low key. He has resources of attitude. On one occasion a guide showed me that in half-a-dozen words he could reduce me to the size of a postage stamp – but his medium altogether lacked this power.

At first of course the pupil himself is less concerned with the long term and much more with his immediate problems, but almost from the start the teacher is working on both levels, upon the pupil's smaller daily self and also upon his larger, more hidden, part.

In understanding his pupil's problems and struggles he draws close and shares something of his being. Behind his immediate struggles the pupil in a subtle way gradually begins to feel himself aligned to, and part of, a larger landscape. This comes from the influence of the guide's attention.

> The one thing people lack is contentment. That is not satisfaction. That is something that can only become part of one's being by applied effort. Cleansing, cleansing, cleansing: not cleansing the blood, not cleansing the body, but cleansing the mind and enlightening the mind.
>
> If your world could only sense what is being brought individually to those who seek, what a power could be released.[7]

The response he wins arises because the pupil, feeling understood, then becomes more willing to learn. If for instance he is embarked on an entangling love affair, the teacher might comment that the honey on a pair of lips is better than no emotional expression at all; he brings sympathy as well as hinting at limitations. In general he aims at helping a situation to fulfil its purpose before the pupil makes it too late to do so. The course suggested is likely to be gentle, not violent. Full regard will certainly be paid to the value of other persons concerned. Never does the guide see the pupil as isolated from everyone else. There is no room for ruthlessness in his philosophy.

In him, insight and tolerance hold hands. Sometimes the tolerance becomes a remarkable solvent of the limitations; it is a way of love, a pathway in which masculine and feminine ways of loving walk together. Every good marriage, after all, contains something of it.

4

The many mansions of the Bible can be interpreted as interior levels of consciousness. The current mansion is thus as much an expression of limitation as of vision. Whether on earth or 'heaven' we can live only in the mansion we have so far earned.

Hence the need for some assistance. The stream of help from guides and teachers which flows to earth can be looked on as part of the moral economy. Spiritual coinage, like earthly coinage, needs to be kept in flow to be healthy.

> It is important with a fresh inflow of spiritual insight and wisdom that it should be firmly grounded. If man holds it in his heart that he will find the best in the world, he *can* find, and in the finding he finds himself. Because it is good to grow from within, and if we grow from within, we have to radiate without.[8]

We pass it on to others, but not by preaching or finger-wagging. We teach involuntarily and often in a way unrecognised simply by becoming our real self as nearly as we can yet reach it.

Surely, it will be asked, whatever truth there may be in this teaching, many will ask more help from the guide than is healthy. Quite so: it arises whenever the guide is expected to perform what is really our own task.

5

Indeed guides perhaps show their love most when they walk close beside their charges in everyday life. In the beautiful pastoral phrase, they have 'a cure of souls'.

Their simplicity here is sometimes deceptive. A phrase much used by one teacher is 'keep on keeping on'. How trite, how obvious – but does it not anticipate and hopefully forestall the later hesitations and weakenings of purpose once the first impulses have waned? In practice, it is a little less obvious that it is far from meaning 'keep on standing still'. Most guides express the importance of preserving spiritual momentum. 'Be not weary of well doing' is adopted as the frequent phrase of another, and also 'The fields are white with harvest now'. So again no postponement.

Many decide to strike their own bargain with God, one of good and sincere intention. The most common bargain is to promise to carry out the conventional tasks during the seventy years or so on earth, and then receive in exchange life for eternity. If ever there were a bargain basement spiritual proposition this must surely be it.

When man seeks God, he wishes to find God on his terms. He wishes God to come along, as a person, and say: 'Here I am, this is God. Now you will put your house in order, you

will pay your debts, you will be kind to your relations, and this is your code of behaviour for life. And when you live this, you will be alright'. But God does not do that, he does not come as a person, he comes as an unseen presence, and he says 'If you will ask for guidance, the guidance will come through experience.' And then he says: 'you must have pity and you must have wisdom, and you must have kindness, and gradually these things come into your life.' You give sympathy because you see the need for sympathy, and not because of what it is going to do for your evolution – it must be selfless. And then you will find that gradually through these experiences God becomes more apparent. The guidance that comes from our world becomes more obvious, it is inter-penetrating, and the spheres of light become more real to you, and gradually become a transcendental experience. . . . But mankind cannot make progress without being able to translate truth into experience for others.[9]

Guides, besides being tolerant, are also very caring. Few pupils have not at some time seen their guide deeply distressed with humanity's selfishness and ability to destroy both itself and this beautiful earth. But direct reproof is not a guide's way; instead he gives positive indications and suggestions. Thus he is unlikely to say that reserve and privacy are wrong, or that outgoingness is to be curbed. He seldom speaks of right or wrong: he usually gently suggests new ways of looking at things. At times he may come down right beside his listeners and tell of his own past earth faults. Thus a former Mandarin:

When I was on earth, unfortunately I was surrounded by my importance which made it difficult for evolvement . . . which is one reason why you find me still here such a long time later. I am aware of my failings and no longer afraid to look at them or speak of them . . . It is not good for my evolvement to accept too joyfully the phrases of praise you give me. It is right to recognise what you are and have, but it can be most dangerous. One has a little twinge of ego. In my

time I was such a very proud man and it is one of my greatest failings. Even though it was a long time ago, that is all the more reason that I should have forgotten my pride.

I worked all my life to leave my provinces in the most perfect order with all the strings beautifully tied-up to my way of thinking; and it was in such a little time that the winds blew all my ideas away like so much dust on your windows and there was nothing left to show my lifetime's work, which I had thought so highly important and that all the provinces would be in much disturbance without my supreme knowledge and guidance! Of course, nothing of the sort happened. They just went on their way as they always had, and I should have invented my rules to suit their way, but I didn't know that then. That is how life is . . . But I thought at the time that I was very wise. My sense of importance was the one thing I would have done well to have left behind me, for it has weighed upon me and has taken me so long to realise what a stupid old man I was.[10]

6

Guides most certainly lay no claims to great stature. Nevertheless when pressed they admit that they have to 'clothe themselves' with an appearance which will not be too strong for our own degree of consciousness. Pupils come to recognise for themselves, as years of study pass by, that a guide is more than he appears, and that the being he knows is only an aspect, a presentation, only a part of the whole teacher.

It is obviously far more important to practice their teaching than to try to decide their stature. This is impossible for us anyhow. All we can come to know with certainty is that their stature exceeds our own. This becomes more and more self-evident.

In continuous learning, certain spiritual aspects of life

are seen to lie at the edge of vision and gradually come into clearer focus. The teaching of discarnate guides is soaked in reciprocal aspects. As we learn, we insensibly teach; it is impossible to live for oneself alone; as we give, so we receive; as we receive so must we give, or the source of receiving will dry up. To inherit the hardship of earth is not a punishment, or an injustice, but a valuable path of learning. To trust life in the right way is one of the constant lessons; this can involve waiting to find out more; making oneself in fact available to be taught. All virtues are gifts to others; all vices are a grasping for the self.

In the early stages then the guide's kindly words are addressed to the everyday part of the pupil. But behind the easy meanings, the pupil's inner mind is also being touched.

The teaching is always simple. But to understand the simplicity can be difficult and sometimes costly. The guide speaks simply because he has learned to be simple in himself – he has learned the purity which resides in it.

If you tell a group of men that in ordinary life only about 10 per cent of the brain is in use, and promise ways of making conscious use of more, it will probably be thought of in terms of self-advantage, of one-up-manship. What will result is highly likely to be an ego-trip, but the guide is not interested in ego-trips. Even in spiritual matters, man too easily thinks of saving his skin, of cultivating his own garden. It is a natural habit spreading from everyday attitudes, but totally alien to the true inner self. Spiritual qualities are the only real assets in the long run. A guide's introduction to an intensified inner life is thus likely to be accompanied by very simple suggestions. Sometimes they will seem so simple as to be obvious, and being obvious the student can think them near to being meaningless. He may be bored, because sure that he knows it already.

This is the secret. Love your life; be kind to your body, to yourselves and be kind to each other. It sounds like Sunday School talk, but it is profound cosmic truth . . . You hear so much that the key is in the human heart and it is love, that these words become platitudinous. But when you awaken to the truth, to the word love, it is no longer a platitude. It is life; it means that the life within your being has begun to grow and blossom and fruit.[11]

In the words of another teacher:

We have to pass through the doorway called self. The doorway of self has a very strong door, because each person clings to their individuality and their personality, and each thinks that door is theirs, not realising the doorway of self is to go through. It is so massive that no strength will move it until we realise that if that doorway is self, all we have to do is to give ourselves away. Give yourself away, not in abasement or mock humility, but in service and that doorway will go. And this is what we tell the aspirants; we say, do not clutch on to 'I must do this' – it must be voluntarily done. There must be a dawning awareness that before entering into this next state of being voluntarily it is necessary to say 'I am no longer needing the self' and the doorway will vanish and light will come through.[12]

7

After death each person's innermost thoughts and feelings are open to be seen by all those around him. He cannot but be seen as he really is. It is not possible to hide away true motives.

Many who came over were those who were in monasteries and nunneries, who thought that their lives were good and holy and pure, but they had not realised that the unconscious parts of their nature were not as smooth and as even and as

44

whole as they hoped. And there has been much repression of many longings and aspirations. When they came to our world, they saw what they did not know – they are not to be blamed – but this is what we say, this knowledge can teach mankind that the unconscious parts of his own nature are still present when he comes over here, and in their own shape and form condition his environment.[13]

What a guide is aware of is the pupil's true nature, though his attention is not necessarily conscious of trivial outer facts. He is not concerned with these. To see the pupil's inner self as all see it after death forms one of his working tools.

He consequently sees where, within the total picture, the pupil's next effective spiritual step lies. Outwardly he may seem to be making things more difficult for the pupil, but inwardly he is making things easier. His extended knowledge is important because objective; often he foresees what is bound to work itself out through circumstances, perhaps seemingly fortuitous, which will later arise to confront the pupil more and more closely through his own difficulties of character. His skill lies in helping the student to overcome the blocks and resistances of which he is only dimly aware. Sometimes the student (as the modern phrase goes) does not want to know. The guide puts things in ways which he thinks the student will most readily come to accept. He speaks in a positive and encouraging way. He is no accuser or bringer of doom. He finds it positively unpleasant and even difficult to judge traits in a negative way. The qualities the student has so far failed to express in his life are seen rather as lacking, as yet, the true shape and beauty they will ultimately display when he becomes more of his true self.

In the early days the student is inclined to think that the guide's powers are almost limitless and that his job is to wave some sort of magical wand to help him. But the

work is wholly rooted within the spiritual law. The guide knows far better than the student when it is necessary to bow before it. This involves withholding help at times, when he sees that more will be learned by struggling alone.

Another aspect of the magic wand syndrome is for the pupil to expect some brand new quality to be added to him. He may, for example, expect a degree of psychic development to come his way, without his doing any real work to gain it. Much more likely to be required however is a refining and purifying of existing qualities. It is no easy task to observe faults, so readily displayed and observable by others, but to which he himself is blind.

> Truth can only come when people are ready to receive. Often they want to dilute truth and put it into their own formula, and make it something they can accept. You have to work to find truth.
> Our words are more than the words you hear, they have hidden instruction.[14]

The true working material therefore lies within the pupil himself. The garden needs more intensive cultivation than has so far been provided. The guide's influence is far from the soft option often supposed. If it is said that no guide exists, and that the pupil is really listening to his own injunction, the guide is not likely to object to someone else's opinion of his non-existence. His task very much includes helping the pupil to listen better to the self-knowledge already hidden within him. Meanwhile he sometimes has to be the spokesman for it. Radical reorganisation may gradually arise. Like charity, the process has to begin at home, and work on present possessions or 'mispossessions'. Moral bonfires are fine when it is one's own, now worthless, possessions one is burning.

46

So the guide offers no weak and pleasant acquiescence in the pupil's everyday self, but nor is he the strident martinet the person selling morality so often becomes. With his broader humanity he brings his gentle power of interpreting the pupil to himself. The relationship – in spite of inherent difficulties of communication – is an entirely natural one, a combination of ease and effort which good temper in the pupil, particularly towards himself, will enable him to enjoy.

> Analysis is good, but love is the best criterion. And if love is flowing and there is a true communication, wisdom flows also, and the strength from our world revitalises and restores.[15]

All being well the student gradually becomes the friend and then the ally, and later the fuller companion. He recognises more and more that he and the guide are spiritually at one, and remain at one through each deepening step on the way.

To the teacher every man is a spiritual being linked alike with other humans and with those in the inner world. As such he is also a particular and unique creation of the God-force. This is not hazy idealism but an everday working concept. Men themselves at a very basic level sometimes find themselves recognising something of this linking, hardly knowing how, as when opposing military forces meet in truce, or police and pickets, their content over for the day, relax into a rough but good-humoured comradeship. They cannot keep up the pretence. On the other hand serious spiritual crimes arise through religious oppression or social pride or greedy exploitation, or when men are treated as slaves or outlaws or chattels or as numbers in an inventory. It happens whenever inhumanity overcomes relationships.

The most fundamental tenet of the teaching is that,

rightly understood, the universe, however appearances seem totally otherwise, is benevolent alike to mankind and all the orders of nature which live within it. Whether in nature or in human life, death is quite otherwise than seems on the surface, and not the spectre so often depicted. It is as much a birth as a death. This is reflected in the true title of the Egyptian *Book of the Dead* – the *Book of Coming Forth by Day*. Discarnates by their very existence share with us the basic peace this brings. They attempt thus to remove the desperate scramble and scurry which prevents men from living to the full. They ask us to allow life to show itself to us more as it really is below the surface. They convey their own security.

Whether the guide speaks by outer communications through a medium, or by a deepening process of private inner communion, wherein with infinite patience he tries over and over to make an impact upon his pupil, it is like the sunlight caressing a bud until it is no longer too green and tight to open. What he says will perhaps well up into the heart and mind only years later. 'Why have I not thought of that before?' Why indeed?

Sources of Quotations

1 to 9   From private teachings
10   *Teachings of the Mandarin* pp. 159–60, 170
11   White Eagle Lodge: a private teaching
12 to 15   From private teachings

CHAPTER FOUR

MULTI-LEVELLED MAN

1

A GREAT DEAL of the spiritual path lies in putting one's own house in order. That makes it unpopular. The work however cannot be avoided. Guides hope by use of their wider background to show more of the meaning of our own lives – emotional, philosophical, spiritual – for they assure us we already belong to a larger concourse than we recognise. What they tell us is not intended at all as a final statement which once heard establishes the facts for good. It is a glimpse only of a living whole but one which enables us to change ourselves as we gradually absorb fragments of it which are within our reach.

Take 'heaven' for instance; a concept which a thousand earnest sermons have done little to enlarge. The main obstacle is when heaven is looked upon as an achieved and total state. The train, so to say, has reached the buffers of our final destination. In the fuller discarnate picture there is nothing of this at all. Instead there is a picture of ever-expanding consciousness; to reach each stage involves both an achievement and a casting off, a shedding of limitations only then perceived as such, and a constant expansion into an unknown. The ultimate

49

perfection, all guides say, is so far ahead as to be also totally beyond their own understanding.

> We in our realm, and in a little more enlightened state, still have problems that we have to resolve and they are heirs, as it were, obstacles to truth and progression until we can overcome ourselves and what we want, and accede to the divine will.[1]

At certain times, in reaching upwards into the unknown, part of what is said is perceived instantly as transparent truth; sometimes there is an overplus, hard to grasp; vanishing almost as it comes. The overplus is likely to contain a gift of love and insight towards us, at once personal and impersonal. We are being invited to grow into a hidden part of ourselves. The unknown in the guide is speaking also to the unknown in ourselves.

> Find how to understand the interpenetration of the planes of thought. We ask you not to let yourself be tied in any way by the ideas that men have already expressed, to allow us to infiltrate into your consciousness to a point where you know without words.[2]

It is a little easy for certain temperaments to come to believe they are becoming almost too good for earth. The brute fact is more likely to be – and certainly this whole machinery of communication and teaching supports it – that very few of present mankind rise much above the level of their own personal tasks. Even the mystic who far surpasses this, who has been profoundly influenced and indeed changed forever, cannot recapture his vision at will. For many of his days it is beyond him. It is as if life holds him down to earth and that this is a very healthy process.

The present limited objective of guides is to awaken men, one by one, to a wider framework of being, to bring about a deeper spiritual participation, the arousal of a

common purpose for the amelioration of earth. Because this objective is shared with those on earth, and has to be partly carried out by them, these teachers often say that they need us as we need them.

Guides are obliged to work then in accord with the possibilities they see. After the preliminaries, the pupil will probably find himself drawn into some group work. It is clearly considered an essential factor in his training to learn to work steadily in this way, with discipline, punctuality and perseverance, requiring and expecting nothing for his own benefit. A group for spiritual healing is very suitable.

Later he is likely to find himself in a further group where he can receive more closely-knit teaching than is possible in public meetings. It is a rule that in any meeting those least familiar with the teachings are afforded prior attention. The pace has to be that of the slowest. Thus entry into a private teaching group is usually extended to those who have already received a degree of training. This prevents the teacher having to go over old ground so often. However, one who claims through membership an elitist role simply shows that he has not at all absorbed the spirit of the teaching. Focussed upon himself, he is on the contrary holding back the rest of the class.

Later, pupils may be invited to receive a deeper layer of teaching. At such a time some of the outer events of life often alter. He or she is confronted with the need to deal with events through new qualities to be both learned and practised. The pupil is put to the event. It must never be thought that a guide's work is only in the classroom. What the pupil does in his everyday self will be under private and loving observation and when life offers a reproof, the teacher refrains from doing so too.

It is a fair axiom that the more closely-knit the group, the greater will be the call upon the pupil. Complacency is

one of the deadly enemies. In a closely-knit group, working say, for world peace in a directed mental harmony, pupils are sometimes given a spiritual name. This may seem rather thrilling, but there is a catch. The name probably points directly or indirectly to a spiritual quality. What the pupil does not know is whether this describes one of his best-earned qualities or whether on the contrary it is one of which he is greatly in need. At first sight, it looks easy enough to know the difference; whether one has, or has not. By no means. The perception of a spiritual quality is a subtle matter, and the conferring of the name can itself offer a lesson in spiritual discrimination.

The overall pictured painted is not at all to be looked upon as a rival one to set against the orthodox Christian view nor against those conveyed in other great world religions. It is more a contributory picture to a whole which is composite and always incomplete. The Christian picture itself exceeds and cannot be contained within everyday orthodoxy. It is much more a part of a mystical statement, a mosaic with many fragments contributed by the individual insights of saints, holy scholars, and intellectually daring pioneers.

Guides are happy for their picture to take its place alongside others. To them any path is equally good if it is leading the student onward. A current phrase proclaims that 'life is for living'. This sometimes amounts to no more than a way of saying that life has no moral values, so one is free to live how one thinks one wishes. Discarnate teachers use the phrase in a very different sense. To them to live is to learn, and the best way to learn is to use what life is teaching us through living with every insight we can reach. The Lord favoured David, who loved much and lived fully. Love is giving and sharing, not taking, though right and gracious taking can also have much in it of giving.

Guides accept one as one is, and do not demand standards of behaviour that one is as yet unable to reach. Life, as one's tutor, will have brought fruits of experience whether for good or ill, which most certainly continue after death within the character created. Results are decisive but never irrevocable or without second chance. Guides look upon this latter as a man-made idea, degrading and unfeeling. Certainly earth events bring consequences but also the chance of living through the consequences and of ameliorating them, once one's former actions, whether before or after death, are recognised in their true light. One is shown the correction needed; if refused or delayed the resulting consequence is a further smallness and limitation in one's own character. This continues until one amends oneself. Ample encouragement will be given, together with patience and sympathy for the predicament. That is one way discarnate teachers have of giving love. Their patience proceeds from love.

In day to day experience most lessons which life offers are at or close to one's present spiritual level. There can be abrupt ones of crisis, but more often they are gradual and subtle; the weeding out of selfishness and weakness, part of which may need very deep and persistent attention to detect at all. All this forms the battleground which students so often see as an irksome limitation. Guides have another and more joyous name for it; they welcome it as *blessed* limitation. It is blessed because it concentrates the outer man on the tasks of the older inner man he bears within him.

Love sets men free from their lower selves. They must first lose life, their lower one.

There are many deaths in our world, they are aspects of being, and there are many deaths to the lower self that have to be killed off in the earth life; it is easier in the earth life.

Why do people gather to themselves things, because when they come over to us it is even more difficult for them to detach themselves from that greed of possessing.[3]

2

Behind the teaching directed particularly to each pupil, lie the simple pillars appropriate to all, forming the basic construction.

The first pillar is undoubtedly the one proclaimed by Jesus the Christ; to love God and one's neighbours as oneself. This underlies all. The second pillar; as one receives so one must give in return. The third pillar; the significance of one's personal lot however seemingly hard is part of a complete spiritual plan for one's ultimate well-being. The fourth pillar; to learn to live as best one can more fully, both in one's own being and in more of life. The fifth; to accept a profound presence at work, a mysterious life-force which plays upon all that is around us and within us.

These pillars are interpreted by guides in terms of 20th century life as we know it. They can be expressed very simply. What is simple however can be very difficult to act out. Guides prefer the simple course as the most effective. They are naturally well aware of subtleties, as their words make clear. Subtleties in the wrong place and with wrong motives confuse and mislead. No guide is ever ashamed of being simple.

He will never accept that one good deed or good quality can cancel out a different bad one. Each has to be accounted for separately. Bad remains bad until it is remedied. Morality is looked upon as essentially so simple that every man can come to see and know it within himself.

'The most effective brother is the one who loves the most.'[4]

If a man loves God and his neighbour, he already has the best guide to what is right or wrong. He is on the way to a life more abundant. When morality becomes confusing or puzzling, the guide is likely to teach how to be more honest with oneself. Honesty and the voice of conscience are very close to one another.

Since all are governed by limitation, blessed or otherwise, it can be argued that error is unavoidable. Certainly we are not called upon to be all at once admirable moral all-rounders. The more simply and honestly a moral limitation is looked at, and the less it is excused and justified, the sooner the remedy is likely to appear. The student gradually finds that the price he is paying for any limitation becomes no longer worth it; then he will look for what best to put in its place, and it will loosen its hold upon him.

When he thus truly faces his own imperfections, a deep peace gradually arises. This peace is one of the keys which guides seek to impart. It can be felt both in their words and in their presence. It is perhaps their most valuable gift to us. A deep sense of presence is described too by some communicators not long after their death, in an enhanced form. This is well pictured in two independent accounts, one received in America and the other in England.

The first is from George Whitby, a Unitarian minister whose death was in 1980.

> Certainly there is the most gentle penetrating wise and tender guidance, and not necessarily from beings you see or know. Rather, an all-pervading presence or presences.[5]

The second is claimed to be from William James, the well-known American psychologist and psychical researcher.

> Everywhere I sense a presence . . . like a loving condition that permeates existence . . . That magnificent good intent is strangely combined of impersonal and personal elements, of this I am sure . . . I sense a deep understanding on its part of my subjective reality, a comprehension that far exceeds my own understanding of myself. On the other hand, if I were someone else, this intent would be just as powerful and as personally directed. Indeed, everyone with whom I have come into contact feels in the same relationship to this atmospheric presence as I do. This same atmospheric presence and knowing light also sustains earth . . .[6]

Thus an important part of what discarnates are teaching is that our nature is grounded in exactly the same God force as theirs. As we refine our own inner experience we find our way closer to this peace.

> What is your duty? No, we won't use the word duty. What is your opportunity? It is so simple. Give yourselves time every day to relax your physical activity, and attune your consciousness to the enfolding and inflowing light and love of the Great White Spirit. It is through the individual awareness of the great love permeating all creation and all mankind that the world will come to the new golden age.[7]

3

Teachers see spiritual relationships on earth as irrespective of ties of blood or their absence.

Blood relationships are part of the outer machinery of living; they can be very close, or of comparatively little importance. Many come to feel that some members in the family into which they are born are fundamentally strangers, if dear strangers. Within human relationships and groupings, different levels of spiritual reality can be intertwined. The mother may relate with great significance

to one child, yet very much less so or hardly at all to another, his brother. The brothers themselves, forming a different grouping with one another, can be close or distant therein.

In a long established family, with its own tradition, fostered over the generations, duties can become laid on members of a later generation who spiritually do not belong to it. In other cases the tradition can press hard on members who accept its tasks but for whom it is a sacrifice, willing or unwilling. The entail, for instance, can be a hard taskmaster. So can illnesses, cares, need to support. The family structure is one mechanism to introduce life tasks by way of imposed obligations, met perhaps in very different mood, or with very different grace. It can produce come-uppances which otherwise would not have reached us so appropriately and effectively. Other family situations of course are humdrum and of limited value. Whether in terms of family, or through quite different deep relationships formed elsewhere, obligations can arise and be lightly assumed which then tighten around one, or others where a spiritual opportunity, lying hidden, goes unobserved or is lightly cast aside. But the very closeness of family situations gives opportunity for spiritual situations altogether beyond obligations of blood; they can bear, too, insidious temptations of commission or omission. Similar depths of course can also exist in life situations away from the family, where the outer structure is less tight, and the spiritual opportunities just as strenuous though less obvious.

Since they look at earth life from the inside, teachers often point to more important perspectives than the obvious one. If we look too exclusively at the outside there is risk of beguilement, bringing what they call a wasted incarnation.

With such a perspective it is readily seen that fixed moral codes can be too inflexible to embrace all the inner realities. Despite their excellences they are not proof against the gradual crystallisations, hardenings and rigidities which overtake most earth activities. As, for instance, when the battle is lost because generals devised their strategy upon what succeeded in the previous war, or in businesses which well serve one generation but then find their former wares of waning interest to the next. Not many today buy a packet of pen nibs!

Teachings from the discarnate world seek a flexibility which will not fall quite so easily into rigid affirmations; as well as the great simplicities they honour a principle of change and growth. For example a hundred years ago the searching conscience of the Rev. Stainton Moses wrote down discarnate teachings aimed at shaking some of the religious certainties of his time and bringing about a loosening of Victorian orthodoxy including his own. Later, the emphasis fell more on post-mortem experiences, as in R. J. Lees's trilogy, where can be seen a gradual shift away from conventions and towards value-experiences arising closely within the human heart. Conscience took on new values thereby. Later again a more inward and subtle set of values has been introduced, with much less emphasis upon the narrow immediate upshot of one personal life, and more instead upon a longer span.

4

With so far for mankind to go, the guides declare that lessons designed for earth cannot possibly all be learned in one short spell of seventy years. Therefore it necessarily involves a process of reincarnation. They see

life as geared to give every person the most appropriate opportunities for overcoming former problems as they gradually present themselves once again. Reincarnation forms a central pillar in their teaching. They see much of it as a tool used on a long term basis to teach the individual. Much virtue, they declare, is only acquired very gradually and with much effort, trial and error. They see man's task as not to seek out a fixed heaven but more to live out again and again, alternately on earth and in the thither world, spiritual values likely to be mastered only extremely slowly. Against this background all men are essentially equal, each a creation, an emanation from the God-force which will eventually bring to realisation its own full potential. In search of his as yet hidden self man at the same time is in a very real way in search of God.

> In my halting way I am trying to convey to you in a word many things that a word cannot convey, that have to be spiritually discerned and spiritually taken in and built into yourself.
> This is our ideal, what we are trying to convey to you – practical mysticism.[8]

It can then be seen that no man in his essence can be exalted above another. There is a pregnant maxim – no man is your friend, no man is your enemy, each man is your teacher.

In the same way, to discarnate eyes, masculine and feminine values are of equal merit; in their differences each sex comes to see the virtues of otherness and sets out to create the perfect partnership. We come to discern, as most depth psychologists teach, that men and women are essentially bi-sexual in nature. Eventually perhaps as the long journey winds deeper and deeper into the inner worlds, each will become equally man and woman in himself or herself. This touches here on mysteries beyond

present reach: the real meaning of the doctrine of the hermaphrodite is hinted at but not as yet revealed. The bi-sexual nature has also obvious implications as to reincarnation; what more natural than that in one life the masculine and in another the feminine aspect should take temporary precedence, the spiritual lesson of one aspect giving place to the lessons of the other aspect, until in the distant future the rounded whole is wrought?

Reincarnation, as will be seen in a later chapter, brings into harmony many puzzling aspects in the complex and tortuous tale of human relationships, often, when without a key, so hurtful, painful, inexplicable or seemingly pointless.

5

In the gradually emerging discarnate picture man becomes seen then as a multi-levelled being, with nothing like the whole of himself able to be expressed or experienced within his present mortal frame. His real stature is greater than he can yet know. In that sense the present story of life after death is and has to remain incomplete, because we cannot understand more of this fullness.

In listening to and unravelling the picture, an important part lies in the refusal of teachers to say they are giving us the whole truth. They teach us part of the whole. To be greedy for more, or even to supply it for ourselves as best we can, is bound to lead to self-delusion. Guides seek to save us from ourselves. They see mankind as heavenly children in earth clothes.

The primary heresy in this area of temptation is, not surprisingly, to be confident we know more than we really do. At the most shallow level are the self-proclaimed

expositors, that somewhat pitiful area where pseudo-knowledge confidently pontificates. In other spiritual schools too it is painful for teachers to listen to pupils of good-will expounding on their behalf what they have never said. It is a cross the discarnate teacher knows he must bear. Why not correct it? But as one teacher patiently remarked, 'Error is always right in its own estimation'.

Essential too to the meaning of the teaching is that man's function is not to flee life, but as far as he can to enrich it, and that the tools to do so lie to his hand. As man learns to make himself more whole, so he makes and finds life more abundant.

> The consciousness we are seeking . . . like waves on the shore, comes slowly and surely to those who seek and seek and thirst, and . . . when the wave touches you, then it is left with you for always, you do not lose it.[9]

An early lesson is to give reassurance to the pupil that he faces his continuation after death in a world which he need not fear beforehand, and that earth life and the life which follows it are governed alike by the same law of love.

The pupil, looking at the present life around him, very much doubts that this can be so.

Why he need have no fear is that wherever he stands and however depraved he may be, he will never be condemned; it is always made possible for him to extricate himself, and to move up to the next state of consciousness beyond his present one. Unlimited help is available; the only governing factors are his willingness to receive and to act accordingly, to begin to flow with the tide of spiritual law instead of against it.

The concern and love from a teacher who is taken (mistakenly in fact) to be a stranger, is much more

important than the production of a few striking evidential facts the effect of which can wear off or become subjected to carping doubt. Spiritual law as teachers say, works gradually. They never work for a forced growth. Such a plant, in their eyes, will be etiolated and weakly.

6

Each person knows inwardly when he is doing violence to his own nature and departing from his inner self. In spite of the quasi-convincing intellectual super-structure, or the plain obstinacy which he relies on sometimes to prove to himself he is right, something in him knows otherwise. His inner nature, lost or partially lost, in spite of all, speaks with a true voice.

The spiritual law gradually possesses one, as one gives up outer daily perturbations in order to make room for it. No true way of life exists without renunciation as part of it.

> The whole process is one of learning how to let go, and how to cleanse yourself of all the unworthy things.[10]

Long before a man takes the decisive but often gradual step upon the true spiritual journey, the values which formerly sustained his life have begun to lose their nourishment and pleasure. These include the easily-won everyday satisfactions.

It does not at all do to regard everyday values as appropriate to earth, and the level of consciousness next above it to be appropriate to life after death. This is to make a false and artificial division, and a comfortable one at that. These new levels need to be recognised as valid on earth. When accepted, they will bring about a degree of transformation, in which the inner man gradually takes over from the outer; and, far more important, by the

process of individual transformation, earth life too is itself being gently and indefinably transformed. It is the working of the leaven, but the man does not bring it about; he makes himself available for it. It then spreads, beyond him, an influence of which he will be largely unconscious. He is not at all likely to achieve it by thrusting upon his neighbour what he thinks will be good for him. This is how his former level of consciousness chose to work.

Often an apparent tension appears between immediate commonsense and spiritual law. Basically a tension of consciousness, this is resolved when it becomes clearer and clearer that spiritual law takes precedence. Spiritual sense then begins to be recognised as commonsense also. Spiritual sense can be so simple that the simplicity itself produces difficulties. It is hard indeed to trust to what is spiritually simple. That after all has been the challenge of Christianity; men say its simplicity makes it too hard to live it.

Between the spiritual journey and the ego-trip the essential difference is clear. The man engaged on an ego-trip is concerned to enhance the self he knows on earth; he seeks to gain more for it. The man on the spiritual quest finds in time the need to give himself up and to seek nothing in return here or hereafter. Reward is a word which disappears from his vocabulary, though gratitude does not.

Sources of Quotations

1 to 3   From private teachings
4   White Eagle Lodge: a private teaching
5   Rev. G. S. Whitby (posthumous)
6   *After-death Journal of an American Philosopher*, pp. 169–70
7   *Stella Polaris*, February 1985
8 to 10   From private teachings

CHAPTER FIVE

ENTRY INTO THE INNER WORLD

1

VERY MANY PEOPLE already acknowledge and work with some fragment of their inner self, and would regard life as much impoverished without it. Indeed it is a blissful moment to recognise the first indubitable contact. One then also becomes more readily aware of its presence in other people. They are seen in one context or another to be spiritual peers and comrades. Though there may be no shared activity, what is established is a kind of inner freemasonry, part of the spiritual brotherhood of life; to find oneself, as Myers was fond of quoting, to be one of 'this blessed band of brothers'.

By its very nature the inner self cannot live only for itself. Sharing and brotherhood are of its essence. Sharing however belongs at both recognised and unrecognised levels. The guide – and the title is well-named here – endeavours to reveal to one also a little of the more distant part of one's inner self. This does not so much belong to one, as one belongs to it.

It is sometimes at first found in the most mysterious part of our memory. Somehow, however dimly, we know of its existence. If it is said also that we have forgotten much about it, we begin to touch the mystery.

This sense of having forgotten can be touched off at times, at an intense moment of living, as when following the sudden catastrophic death of her much beloved daughter Rosamond Lehmann found herself taken up momentarily into an altogether higher level of experience.

> Awestruck, astounded . . . And yet the sense of recognition, recollection, was predominant. Again and again I told myself: 'Yes. This is reality. I had forgotten'.[1]

Within something of the same area, can be an instant release of spiritual energy, perhaps brought about by a deeply attuned spiritual healer.

> I had difficulty at first in quietening my own mind. Then quite suddenly I seemed to be in a different dimension entirely, sexless yet loving and completely understanding, and full of light. But the most wonderful thing of all was that it was RECOGNITION. I found myself saying: 'Of course, *of course*. I had forgotten!'
>
> When I got up, I was so filled with energy that I could have tackled any job of any kind, whether I normally disliked or liked it. This also helped me to understand why this healer was so successful with various forms of paralysis. My super-energy lasted all that day. I went down to the exercise room and danced, and did gymnastics alone, hard, and gradually returned to a more normal state.[2]

Or there can be a direct dream memory of a recently died friend:

> In the dream I went to visit her in what seemed to be a hospital. I said 'How lovely to see you. I thought you were dead!' She laughed. 'Only recuperating. I'll soon be out and well, and remember', and she spoke very earnestly, '*this* is the reality, *this* is the reality.'
>
> I could not, and did not, grieve for her at all after this.[3]

65

Experiences like these cannot be commanded. The inner self in one aspect is the repository of all that has befallen one. In its totality there lies all past memory. The problem is to recover such part of it as is of present value.

Once a part – a near part – of the inner self is recognised as in some degree a working partner in everyday life, deep problems of values arise. Take for instance a doctor who occasionally, at the instant the patient opens the door, finds himself confronted with a clear intuition of what the illness is. It goes against his whole training to act upon anything but an objective clinical diagnosis. It is easy to say that all he needs to do is to test the intuition against the clinical indications; but in that case where is the need for intuition? And supposing the two don't agree, can he always be sure the intuition is wrong? The problem is: to what level does the intuition have access? It is likely that if he treats the intuition as representing a second class citizen at work within him, then in time it will lessen, become less sure, and largely vanish. But what if sometimes at least the inner self shows itself as a first-class citizen? Such a doctor faces a very difficult dilemma of integrity, to bring the two together in an honourable partnership when either half is likely to be found to be wrong at times.

To listen to the inner self therefore requires a certain delicacy of touch which is hard to describe; one gradually learns by the quality of one's own response what best to accept and what best to refuse out of the intimations, which may truly come from within, or may merely crowd in from irrelevant sources, some of them from the everyday self.

A practical difficulty is that in most adults a willingness to learn is not common when uncomfortable areas of one's being are involved. Here an attempt to hold steadily on to a longer vision is called for, since in everyone there

exist undeveloped strands of character, the true nature of which are sometimes hard to recognise. They can need fostering.

Clearly the guide's part in helping the pupil to shape himself is both personal and impersonal, and necessarily so. The reward for the guide does not lie in the love for him which awakens in the pupil; it lies in the pupil's growth of independent spiritual vision.

It is not uncommon for such an inner relationship to be first despised as a soft and weak handing over of one's own decisions, and as an altogether unworthy option. The relationship is much more taxing and demanding than the despiser imagines. To use a light-hearted analogy some professional footballers once agreed to take part in a male ballet class. To their amazement they found themselves too weak to perform a number of the dancer's movements; they simply had not developed the particular muscles needed. The inner world, like ballet movement, is delicate but powerful.

A guide encounters subtle problems of stature; in order to reach the student he is sometimes obliged to dwarf himself, somewhat as parents dwarf themselves so that their child shall understand their words.

The guide has a very clear picture of the oak-to-be which lies within the pupil. The tall oak can be likened to an archetypal image of the full man, implanted in him in embryo by the God-force at his original creation, but needing the experience of many lives to reach its full reality, each brief earth life (and each temporary sojourn beyond) nourishing and correcting some aspect of the whole. An earth life then is no more than a season. Parts of the total manifestation wait for further lives: the vehicle is not yet ready for them. The part on earth meanwhile longs for the fullness of himself he cannot yet reach. The very longing spurs him on towards goals which

he senses but cannot yet accomplish. His life is like a language in which he can only stammer but cannot yet be articulate.

Much on earth then is to enable the filling-in of gaps in oneself, the former potentials not realised, the errors which took their place. That is one part of why we often feel our present earth life so incomplete and so humbling. The other part of the loss lies in buried memories of attainments in earlier lives from which we are now temporarily shut off in order to concentrate on what at present is more important to deal with, the laggard side of one's nature. In very many religions, life is rightly looked on as a school.

2

Many however are reluctant at first to believe that unknown realms of being can exist within them. Some may feel fear of what will be demanded as the more strenuous inner self is gradually found. They probably consider they are making more than enough effort already. Others on the contrary feel altogether too elated at the prospect; these are the ones likely to think they have won this new knowledge long before they have really done so. They become inflated. This is one of the risks in the pupil's imperfection.

Within the inner self a power of hidden direction brings an intensification of the moral nature. Then a duty, an urge, is felt beyond cold and prudent reason, a categorical imperative to which the self, in its deepest part, knows it should accede.

The inner self has two aspects; the more local part which comes to grips with the earth self, and a larger part which knows its true allegiance to be elsewhere. The

psychologist, Mary Scott, uses here the valuable metaphor of senior and junior partner. This expresses very well the nature of the relationship. The senior inner self possesses the insight required by the junior self. Senior and junior partner are not to be looked on as separate individuals; they are better regarded as aspects of consciousness linked at deep levels.

The natural and best way of relating to the senior partner is by continual commitment to, and honouring of, the promptings of conscience. This does not mean using the pedestrian part which does no more than give recognition to socially accepted morals, often grown stale and lacking immediate insight. What is looked for is a more athletic area, lithe, sensitive and resourceful, recognised to be a clearly superior level of insight.

In a very firmly fixed way most men and women look upon themselves as a separate, single unit, responsible for their own fate; a closed unit. This is intensified when the fear of judgment is instilled by priests into their flocks. In the deeper discarnate teaching however, the individual is not regarded as closed but as open-ended. It presents the self on earth as this fragment of a larger whole.

Many have felt in their best moments that they are taken over by a deeper skill and insight than their own, and that their task is to allow themselves as fully as possible to be an instrument. For such brief moments, the self comes together, is enabled to be as one. At lesser moments the junior inner self, pinioned within the clay which is both its prison and its vehicle, mostly obeys its own limitations. It is the reverse of the true alignment, where the total senior self, obedient to its own fullness seeks to harmonise the junior inner self so as best to fulfil the tasks designed in partnership for both. Yet the senior partner is also impersonal. It sees what is, without personal favour or manipulation. It is on these terms that

the relationship is based. The earth part is both protected and limited by the physical density in which it is embedded, away from the more naked thoughts and feelings which must be encountered after death.

Occult accounts have told of encounter with the mysterious figure of the Guardian of the Threshold, terrifying because, whether on earth or beyond, it takes place within this naked self. At this level what it reveals is not to be gainsaid. In one aspect it is the custodian of knowledge of the total past of its charge, over many lives. It is also, quite truly, a part of the self. It might be called the conscience of the whole being, charging the smaller parts of itself both with past crimes and with the tasks which lie ahead. It is the Guardian because until present tasks have been met, the whole being cannot safely enter deeper spiritual realms ahead.

At ordinary earth levels, meetings between inner and outer self are less naked. The heart much more than the mind takes priority. The one on earth is *heartened* to discover more. Gradually the pupil's complaints of his hard lot, or unjust circumstances, become seen in the heart to be opportunities, and not a rod of injustice. With the burgeoning growth of new qualities in the soul, what before looked hostile is now seen as something for which to be grateful. It is almost as if a hand were put forth to offer support to the steps of the one on earth. He feels no longer alone. The less he remains imprisoned in the personal, the more he comes to feel at last at home in the universe.

> Will you please accept life as it is and not reject experiences that may seem harmful and hurtful at times because these are the lessons of living and the lessons of growth.[4]

It is yet another aspect of the wonderful story of the prodigal son.

The senior partner is sometimes described as the higher self. It is a phrase which is hard to free from personality implications, and smacks of spiritual snobbery, even when not so intended. It is better avoided.

Much of the way to the inner self lies in a loosening or a casting off of outer concerns. This does not necessarily imply an ascetic denial either of earthly tasks or enjoyments; what does become renounced is one's attachment to them. One needs to resemble Horatio in taking with equal thanks what life both gives and denies. This is the detachment often urged in occult books, a quality widely misunderstood; it is not chilly, nor unconcerned, nor stand-offish and above all not superior. It is warm and caring, like the good Samaritan who in fact gave an excellent example of true detachment. Having played his part he knew when to move on. It is of little use to regard oneself as a kind of superior spiritual social worker, always ready to poke in one's nose and instantly know better. To share and give of one's own life is much more difficult. It is a question of throwing away both one's isolation and one's over-involvement. Both courses are difficult because there can be no pretences in the world of inner values. Yet in addition to detachment, at a certain stage a right kind of intensity is also required.

The First Degree is that of the Student, the Learner. When the feet set forth and the desire to learn becomes urgent, the student attracts the attention of the great Lords of Karma; they hear his cry: 'I want knowledge; to grow to be of use to God and to the Masters. Make me worthy, O God, to serve!' Then comes the process of purification. The higher vehicles . . . of man need much cleansing, much purification, because much has been gathered into them which hinders and obstructs. Therefore frequently episodes of trouble, sickness, suffering come upon the student; some may be born in a crippled body, endure great tragedy, possibly even commit

crime. The last sounds unlikely, perhaps, but we see beneath the surface. We know this soul perhaps endures suffering and degradation, because of its need of purging. Thus suffering and sorrow, and even separation from loved ones may be the soul's own choice.

The Second Degree is that of the Disciple. The Disciple learns implicit obedience to the Master, to be exact and precise in all his working; no slipshod methods can be tolerated; he works with his 'tools' upon his lower self, shaping and perfecting its frailty and weakness . . . A sincere honesty, an absolute truth is demanded . . . He may deceive none, not even himself, for deception there cannot be in the Second Degree.

The Third Degree is when the Disciple is ready to receive Illumination when he can be trusted with the secrets of heaven . . . Then indeed must he function on the invisible planes without hindrance or limitation.[5]

The spiritual journey is indeed a long one. It is natural to seek rules in the early stages, but rules are not the path, they are an aid to finding where one's own path lies. If the way is not at first found, it remains perfectly acceptable to return to the rules for a while. It is like keeping in good training. In a very real sense, there is no single right or wrong way of advancing, it is a question of recognising where lies the true priority at each moment. Rules and intuition interweave with one another, until the need for rules disappears, calling for a stricter discipline because containing a fuller measure of freedom.

3

The inner world impinges in subtle ways. It lies behind some of the more troubling circumstances towards which we are often so impatient and which if allowed turn out to be wise instructors; not torturers, but more like kind

though firm physicians. If we are unable to pick up these meanings for ourselves, then the guide tells us part, unveiling little by little what we are willing to bear and to use. At other times one's private inner sensitivity, unaided, touches various sources of meaning; valuable hints hidden within outer circumstances or insights gained from former lives and presented again for current use.

Explicit help from the guide, through his deeper knowledge of our circumstances, is also given to encourage us to increase our moral insights into ourselves. Moral worth then often also comes to be perceived in others where overlooked before.

The guide may refer briefly at times to a past life of his own, though rarely, and when given, always for our benefit and not his. If he says he has been an Egyptian priest or a Grecian philosopher, or a humble mediaeval monk, he does not do it to boast, but to stir memories of our own. Such awakening of a slumbering aspect of previously shared discipline comes when it is ready to burgeon again in a new environment. In this brotherhood of the spirit, senior stretches out a hand to junior. The priest or philosopher or monk can mean much to us, but is only a small part of him.

As these inner aspects steal into consciousness the pressures and ambitions of everyday life become of less and less importance, are seen as the childish things which St Paul counselled should be put aside. It is a change of emphasis of great importance. It is not and cannot be a programme; it is a slow and organic response arising at its own pace from deep within.

The inner self, as has been said, is part of a multiple being, holding within its larger memory the essence of all its own previous lives. Deep threads of memory are implanted at birth pointing to the purposes set out to be achieved in this life, together with correction of defective

qualities still within, which brought about earlier failures. In Shelley's words, the soul looks before and after, but instead of sighing for what is not, sets about bringing it into earth existence, as much for others' sakes as its own. Realisation comes that faults damage oneself, but more important, they damage the inner texture of the world as well. A fault in the weaving until put right affects the surrounding strands it touches. In this way one is as fully responsible to the world as to oneself. Out of mercy, and 'blessed limitation', one is spared for the present the full tale of one's past; the burden is too great. Enough is enough to be put right in one life. Other faults remain as a burden for future incarnations, as and when one is fuller in strength to face them.

These are facts to hammer out and make some use of in one's private spiritual workshop. Jung has said, 'The patient does not cure the disease, the disease cures the patient'. It arouses the sufferer's latent spiritual power to find and overcome the interior weakness which drew the illness to him. Life repeats this process of gain out of evil in many ways other than medical ones. We come to sense that trials and penalties, most often the karmic result of former failures, offer behind their sternness of confrontation, a profoundly therapeutic gift to those willing to lay hold of them fully, however deep the stress which such failures bring about.

As we live in blessed limitation, so too the guide accepts an opposite limitation. As we cannot bear our own full being, so also we would not be able to bear his full presence. He is too strong for us, in something of the way that a light can be too strong for the eyes. In fact, quite literally, it is taught that a guide is a being of light, as we ourselves shall become. Hence the shell, or mask, or aspect of himself he adopts, which helps to shield his full light from us. This aspect very probably represents one of

his earlier lives as said above, and a medium is able to describe this limited aspect, but his fuller being remains hidden. Indeed, as some guides say, to drop back into the astral world in order to perform their task somewhat resembles a reincarnation for them, though not into such density as in the physical world. Certainly what we contact is less than the full teacher. Maurice Barbanell has said, after his death, that he has felt uncomfortable when he has found himself in the presence of his guide. Later he felt in awe of him. He realised that in some way he could not yet measure up. Indeed he has also said that the teacher is not as close as when he had worked for him on earth as his medium. That 'business partnership' has ended. The teacher has now discarded the mask he then wore, and is closer to his full self. Many spiritual layers indeed exist in the inner world.

4

Essentially the substance of the teaching apart from its particular mode of presentation is nothing new. It can be found everywhere in the great religions, sometimes in an open form, sometimes more concealed. But it is not in the least a re-hash drawn from an intellectual commonalty of beliefs. Instead it possesses layers of meaning at deepening spiritual levels which, through a process of growth, only come into sight very gradually.

These cannot be gained therefore item by item, as an accretion of knowledge. It is a very common experience on earth that the more one knows, the more one recognises how little one knows. Within this wisdom lies too the principle of discarding. This is part of the growth.

Since what a guide offers is not a regime nor a syllabus he calls instead for response in sensitivity. Learning of a

spiritual kind comes about from an extension in consciousness drawn from the inner parts of the self.

As the pupil struggles with his earth problems and weaknesses, his guide sees him as it were from the inside out. The inner man is much more real than the often ill-fitting outer carapace.

It is useless to expect him, through the person of a medium, to deal with trivial matters, or to give a categorical solution to more important issues which are for the pupil's own decision. The guide, if need be, will stimulate that inner self, but any resulting opposition between inner and outer selves has to be resolved by the pupil. Else he will not grow. When the pupil seeks for the guide to bypass this necessary struggle within him, he is attempting to misuse the situation. He will not succeed either, in exploiting the guide, though he may think he will as when he wilfully stretches advice so as to make it accord with his own wishes. Sometimes the pupil (or non-pupil as better called here) perpetrates this in important matters, with unfortunate consequences. He falsifies the guide's meaning, and, worse, has intended to do so.

To a more earnest pupil it will often seem at first that he can find nothing to focus upon in order to reach more of his inner self. Yet with perseverance an inner conviction arises that there is this *more*. What at first seems as empty as a cinema screen not yet lit, yields to a dimly felt recognition that something within the pupil is waiting to come alive, which is animated partly from elsewhere. On the screen are inscribed one's own true spiritual values, some recognised, others perhaps unwelcome.

To use another image, it is like an intermittent but continuing dialogue of a most intimate kind. The values discussed in the dialogue are not capricious. They come with a gentle but also stern impulse. Even when rejected

their reality is not overturned. This is because inner values are both one's own and also shared with many on earth and beyond. Hence they bring with them an objectivity. They exist independently of the man or woman who perceives them, they are part of the civilisation of the spirit, a culture deeper than one's own. In recognising it, one begins to reach out to it.

This dialogue is of course taking place within the breast of many human beings. It is both composite and individual. Each man can feel he is alone – for only he can accomplish his own task – but at the same time feel and know he is part of a wonderful shared process, partly brought about by a force of mind and spirit beyond his own.

He finds, at first with surprise, that his inner self has an insight superior to that of his daily self. He is gradually faced with seeing some of his old values superseded. There lie within him more sources of perception than he formerly recognised. He sees that these were there all the time, but dormant; his attention was busy elsewhere. He was content with a lower threshold of perception. Now he is waking up to more.

To everyone at times, too, events come to obstruct, sometimes in an altogether adamant way which the one on the path is likely to feel is very unfair. Like Hamlet, he feels this cursed spite, but unlike Hamlet he may not at first at all feel that he is born to set it right. More likely he puts the blame elsewhere.

However, as his own commerce of friendship with his inner self grows and he becomes more familiar with the process of listening and conferring with it, his view of his cursed spite changes slowly also. His accompanying emotions become less unruly. They die down and are replaced by a more enquiring, equable insight, one which brings with it a steadily deepening acquiescence.

5

Like any other discipline, this particular route to the inner self can be trained by utilising various techniques. These are basically very simple; the subtlety lies in dealing with difficulties as they arise in the obstinate outer self.

The most obvious technique is that of meditation.

> Meditation is a place where you feel you want to strip yourself of all the inessentials and second-rate things, and want to be in tune with pure spirit. According to the way you reach out, so you receive that much in return.[6]

Meditation is both simple and difficult. It rests upon the premise that the inner self, though as yet largely unfound, is present and available. This particular mode of meditation has the aim of allowing this inner self to reveal itself. It is something quite other than mere private thoughts. As in many other forms of meditation the need is to slow down the scurrying, bustling self-absorbed outer man, so that its demands gradually drop away.

Successful reception is not achieved by making the mind a blank as so often advised, which usually merely produces tension, but by stilling the outer mind so that the very much quieter voice of the inner self can commence to be heard. Meditation is peaceful. Peace in turn deepens vision and helps to keep it steady. Meditation is a process of a giving and receiving freely within the soul; it is everything that the market-place is not.

In the beginning, and sometimes for a long time, focussing will not be accurate and continuous. Many interruptions are to be expected. What is basically a deepening process of receptivity can become mixed up in a troublesome way when assertive ideas, stirred up within the meditator's own self, impinge, thrusting away the area

where true receptivity lies. Then the loud-mouthed outer self shouts down the voice of the delicately poised mentor within. There are times too when the outer self adds a contribution which seems to blend with the inner voice, but really squeezes it out. This is at first hard to distinguish. It takes time to learn to recognise the two voices with reasonable accuracy. In meditation, as in most areas of living, risk cannot be avoided.

It is often helpful to commence by reading a couple of pages of a spiritual book of which one is fond; but the reading should not be prolonged beyond a few minutes, its intention being simply to allow the mind to sink into itself. It is perhaps helpful to consider the meditation process as akin to telepathy with oneself; preparing oneself and waiting to register the telepathic impression when in its own time it comes about. Its delicate gossamer-like touch comes to be recognised. Often it is non-verbal. It resembles the unmistakable advice of conscience. It registers with a precision and certainty much swifter than everyday dialogue. A meaning presented is instantly recognised as valid. But who recognises it? It is the inner self and it calls upon the outer daily self for assent. When no intimation arrives, patience and serenity are needed. What arises in a meditation cannot usually be foreseen, but nearly always has an immediate application. It can come verbally as a voice, not heard outwardly, but almost as if someone else is thinking his thoughts in one's own head in sentences which form themselves. Here the telepathic process is close to psychic sensitivity.

If an unwelcome intimation is received it does not do to protest, become angry, or rebel, and even less to be self-justificatory. If this happens the outer mind is very obviously intruding and the inner voice is at once disturbed. A household din is not to be tolerated during meditation.

It is not so important as it first seems to know the precise source of true inner material. The validity does not lie in the source but in the content. In the inner world, mine and thine lose much of their meaning; most of what is true is equally mine and thine. Inner truth does not have sharp boundaries. Truth at this level shades gently as it were from one tone-colour to another. In Rudolf Steiner's mystery plays, the stage set for the mental world is a sharp-edged rocky landscape; this is true depiction as a well-known medium once recognised instantly when she saw the stage-set. In the inner spiritual world beyond this mental level all is much more flowing and permeating, merging and parting, as waves of the sea flow together and then separate and then once more return to one another.

Inevitably one's concern often asks, 'Is this thought truly received from elsewhere or is it all my own, no more than my own imagination?' The fear is natural, likewise the concern for truth behind it. Guides say: 'Does it matter where it comes from as long as it is true?' Fruitful ideas in meditation may after all have been implanted beforehand by the guide into some area of the inner self. This raises the further mysterious prospect that we are able to learn things whilst in the sleep state. What is certain is that wherever the source, meditational insight is available at a deeper and more impersonal level than that of the everyday self.

Meditation and its sister, intuition, are very much intended to lead to action. Intuition, so often despised as woolly by the crisp-minded intellectual, has on the contrary the virtue of special precision. At its best, it is in-tuition, or tuition from within; implying that the inner self can possess very direct processes of cognition. Intuition gets a bad name because much is called so which is really no more than wishful thinking allied to

false self-authority. False intuition does not stop to listen; true intuition has already listened and to good effect.

In true meditation certain moral qualities too need to be awake; they provide the nourishing soil in which the meditative process can flourish best. Simplicity (and the intellect too can certainly learn to be simple), humility, purity of vision (which insensitive sophistication destroys) are necessary, as is the especially valuable quality of inner obedience. By this is meant both a listening for the true voice of meditation, and a willingness to accept it. Inner obedience thus combines an attitude and an act. Every spiritual path requires inner obedience; it is part of the natural integrity of the inner self. It also requires a considerable degree of inward attention as well as outer perception. The inner life very much has its own quiet activity.

> We want to take you out of the material world that is pressing so hard on all those who are sensitive to the feelings of others, we want to take you on to the higher planes of being that you might be restored, and your faith in humanity be freshened. Do not be disillusioned, look at each person, who represents truth as they see it at that point, do not condemn, do not judge, but observe, and learn from us, and we will infiltrate into your consciousness the ability to discern, which is the pearl of great price.[7]

> Our thinking, our actions, our deeds have to be such that even if some people make us very cross inside, we must not allow the crossness to be accepted by our spiritual self, we must throw it away and say that is how they look at life but we must love them into understanding; that is more difficult.[8]

81

Sources of Quotations

1   *Swan in the Evening*, p. 115
2   A private account
3   id.
4   A private teaching
5   White Eagle: *Ways of Service* p. 55–6
6 to 8   From private teachings

CHAPTER SIX

REINCARNATION

1

ALL SERIOUS discarnate teachers support reincarnation. If reincarnation is true, this is of central importance, for then a principle of order can be expected to lie within it and to govern it. Causality can then be looked for between one's own nature and the events in life which now surround it, some seemingly so unfairly. What happens cannot confidently any longer be blamed upon a caprice of nature, or the faults of others, or as due to heredity, or to an unjust God. On the contrary, in what happens there will somewhere be a thread related to oneself, both to its present and to some part of its past.

It is a long term portrait of oneself, confronting us from without or from within. It is therefore a source of valuable information, inexorably pointing towards the way it is best for one to go, and showing the obstacles within which obstruct it, because they have obstructed it before. It becomes the fairest and the sternest of our task-masters, yet also the truest friend, telling us what we truly need, and in one part wish, to know of ourselves but have not yet fully faced up to. It is the moving finger which writes, whose words cannot be obliterated. From another aspect it is the long arm of the law reaching out to us from an

earlier life; but more truly the arm is that of our own self.

Reincarnation and the results it has deposited in the inner self thus forms no cosy teaching though it can be presented as being so. It is instead a voice intricately combined of tender conscience and stern realism. It is also a voice of reassurance because it gradually reveals that the faults which beset us do not belong to us in the same close and intimate way as our virtues. All faults are basically misrepresentations, distortions; blind, selfish, or corrupt. Yet when they come into their own and take their true shape they gradually turn into virtues after all, the true meaning of parts of ourselves which have so far strayed, refused, failed in resolve, been obstinate. As in the fairy story the frog turns back into the prince.

2

True reincarnational memories lie hidden in the inner self. Guides teach that these memories do not reside in the physical brain and that this is why reincarnations can seldom be recalled. If reincarnational indications are conveyed through the help of a medium, these therefore need to arouse an inner memory. Recognition at a deep level brings a strengthening from within. So pictures of past selves and the characteristics they reveal can serve as counsellors to the soul. They point down a long road still to be traversed. Or they can act as a wonderful solvent to current disharmonies, both within the present self, and in close relationships. Here again difficult situations can be old ones now presented for a better outcome. The other person, found so difficult, equally has a self-cleansing task to perform. Here patience can provide an important and cathartic role for both.

Turning from this burden of faults and inadequacies inherited from earlier selves, another important aspect arises. Memory of this inner kind is surely not necessarily only of earth lives, but more deeply reflects, as Rosamund Lehmann found, life spans in the interior worlds between one earth incarnation and the next. Such memories are present somewhere, however deeply, in the inner self. Some of the human sense of home-sickness lies here. Each life uncovers a piece of the wholeness of our individual selves.

In one way then it could be perfectly correct to look upon one's present life as one of disappointment and failure, not only through unresolved faults of past lives but also partially reflecting a kind of demotion from our temporary place in the inner world before our present return. The disappointment present however will also reflect the other aspect of demotion, that of the eager willingness felt between earth lives to come back and face present tasks recognised there as essential, bringing a knitting together of the character in an area where weakness failed it before.

In presenting life as an unfinished story, reincarnation teaching also emphasises the permanence of spiritual values. This principle of continuity is very important. It means that lives are not fooling us with false hopes, meaningless felicities, or monstrous and tyrannous punishments but instead are offering for our understanding laws offered over and over for better living until we find the joy of accepting them. Reincarnation is thus a great reconciler. Opportunities it is true can be lost, and the loss can be serious and damaging but it is inevitable that they will come round again, in this life or in the future. The pattern having been laid down, the time needed or taken is comparatively unimportant: we are all still on the way. Nevertheless the time scale involved can

be formidable to contemplate. Yet as an unfinished story, and however long it takes to bring about, the ending is a happy one. Very emphatically reincarnation is opportunity, not punishment. Whatever the appearances suggest, the nature of spiritual life is always positive. The adventure and its worth lie in finding where the positive lies. If if seems deceptive, one's own interpretation will have made the deception. Spiritual law is no deceiver. Time for once is on one's side; in the inner world there is plenty of it.

Reincarnation therefore is not to be regarded as hostile when it brings round again old events which one is reluctant to accept. If the old motivations are still found the inference is clear that there is need for further work until the handicaps formerly brought about within one begin to disappear. It is far from pleasant to recognise that moral disabilities, which one skates over or accepts as normal human imperfections, are really very deep seated. In its positive way, reincarnation teaching assures that the cancers can be dispelled. However, deep-seated faults are often the least evident and the most difficult to accept; the short-sighted, disgruntled rebellious outer personality continues to be ready to dodge its own column.

The spiritual laws expressed in esoteric wisdom make themselves evident in personal life in two main ways. The first is the way of severity; moral laws sooner or later bring moral consequences strictly appropriate to the degree to which they have been flouted. If whisky is drunk to gross excess, the consequences may be, and probably will be, cirrhosis of the liver; but beyond that and much more certainly, a predisposition to excessive drinking – or some equivalent of it – will return to be conquered in a later earth life. Here spiritual law appears as the stern teacher; the pupil's faults if not curbed are allowed to develop their full consequences. The second main

principle is that of mercy and love. Over and over again, opportunities for amelioration are provided, perhaps through apparently chance circumstances, or through a loving relationship, or in the simple healthful effects found in harmony with nature. Various pathways appear, which can mitigate the fault and lead the patient (for that is what he is, however vigorous) back into health. The discarnate guide too is a further influence; behind the scenes his loving attention helps to redeem, if the pupil allows it. These two principles will be recognised by many readers as the twin laws of severity and mercy of which the Kabbalah so beautifully teaches, playing upon each person in intricate alternation. As the pupil deviates to one side or the other, calling into his life the severity or the mercy, each in its separate way invites a return to the centre. They correct his overplus.

Reincarnation, however, is much more than the simple righting of old errors. Rudolf Steiner, in occultly examining Schubert's former history, detected a roistering element in an earlier life. Schubert's syphilis could have resulted from his somewhat similar late-night roisterings in Vienna. The loneliness and exile resulting from this fatal illness are wonderfully expressed in the last six songs of the Winterreise. If no roistering, no syphilis; if no syphilis, no Winterreise, at least in the shape we know. Here, in reincarnation, the spiritual law of compensation can be seen, with its equilibrium and balance. The sin was redeemed in the masterpiece, yet in part brought it about.

From one point of view the working out of reincarnation might be looked upon symbolically, as the inheriting of an estate, much neglected by one's ancestor. One's present self is the true offspring of that neglectful ancestor who, again symbolically, was one's former self, and the estate here is not an ordinary earthly one with its

fields and woods but an interior one, with thickets and twisting paths, and a layout difficult to perceive. Much of what one is now, is what one has been. Man thus has a hidden history. Qualities new or old will be needed to enable him gradually to rebuild the damaged structure. But it cannot be looked on as a simple repair job. Former errors, by the effort now needed to overcome them, have the effect of enriching the remainder which may have become complacent with imagined virtues and which now needs to struggle in order to become leaner and stronger. This is part of 'the law of compensation', and, on a wider basis, part of the immense law which continually creates good out of evil. If regarded rightly, nearly every person, looking honestly, can find how this law has all the time been at work in his life, often in a way not recognised at the time.

The teaching is that evil is held within the hand of the God-force and ultimately is as much a part of that force as what is much more easily recognisable as good. The man or woman who rails against evil both within his life and also beyond it, is railing against the God-force, and is thus really declaring that his own insight could manage things better. An unlikely proposition. Nevertheless, it is of course very, very difficult to look beyond the great evils and tortures all around. Perhaps man needs to raise his stature to find the solution and perhaps sometimes the evil it is which helps to raise the stature.

When the prospect of discovering something of one's own previous lives comes to hand, it is very likely at first to be considered as highly unreliable, or no more than a fantasy. Alleged accounts of former lives are by no means hard to come by. They are on offer through a process of hypnotic regression, or by mediums who specialise in providing such information, based on 'reading' a psychometric object. The recipient then needs to listen

with an inner ear to sense whether or not what is said has any resonance for him. If not he has probably been told of trivial or non-existent lives. Or several lives may be described which really are basically re-tellings of the same life. One suspects too that with no intention to mislead, life situations common to many are likely to be produced in generalised and repetitive form by sensitives who do much of this work without even seeing the recipient. Usually in such stories a fatal flaw shows itself, a total lack of any causality between the lives told about and the present life. There can be no health in reincarnation accounts if they do not offer keys which can be used to unlock present problems. A clear relationship needs to be revealed between past and present, showing up blocks and false stances created by misuse of the self in earlier lives.

To a third person these stories usually seem lame, because in such a listener there cannot exist the answering response, the inner recognition which true stories can arouse in the one to whom they belong. It is this awakening from within that produces the conviction of their reality; the sterner, the less complimentary, the more disconcerting even, the more their truth is likely to strike home. To be told that one has been a good man has little more effect than to produce a yawn. Nor is melodrama in a story of much effect to a careful listener; the quiet thrust is the one which goes home. The thrust however needs to be a surgical one, which however damaging to self-esteem, is bestowed for healing purposes.

In making any serious approach to reincarnation material obviously it is necessary to cast off glamour; stories of oneself in a starring role. Few if any of us of course are likely to have been well known characters. It is an odd quirk in human nature that many would prefer to

have been one of dubious fame or even a villain rather than an ignoramus or a nonentity.

In stories too where ordinary checks on probability are not available there can arise a ready tendency to magnify things. If in a future generation someone is told he once was General Montgomery, the reality may have been that he was no more than a humble sergeant in the Desert Rats. The many who have been told they were once Nefertiti could have been inconspicuous handmaidens in some ancient Egyptian court. However in any earth life there are many boring days. We forget these, and remember the red or black letter days. In the same way lives which overall have been poor in meaning do not make much impact upon the memory. Why should we not virtually forget much of such a life? Some excuse then can be made for claiming colourful memories in one or two lives provided the stern underlying purpose – never far absent – is looked for.

When mediums or hypnotists offer to provide accounts of past lives one has to ask, too, what right do such persons necessarily possess to hand it out? There may be no right of access to a particular set of facts in a past life of their client. There may be good reasons for some facts to need to be withheld. What is appropriate can only be given at the right spiritual hour. When the clock does strike, and information is entrusted, it certainly does not mean that the pupil is more spiritual than another not given such information. Many may rightly be engaged in a life situation where a particular part of reincarnational information is neither necessary nor desirable at this time.

It is hard however to see any overall moral objection to discovering something of our former lives. Loving information encourages us to find how to step away from what we at present are, and to forgive ourselves as well as others. A truthful account will be graded to what the

recipient's guide knows his charge can stand, and is likely to omit what would be too much to bear at present. It can be an act of mercy to recognise that the pupil is not ready to know all of his past. He may still need one or two lives more to grow the moral fibre needed to accept some of his former lives and to begin to put them right.

3

It has to be asked where reincarnational information is obtained from. The usual answer is that it forms part of the akashic records where it is stored for all time. (This is almost certainly a simplified picture of some much more subtle process). Its existence does not imply a right for anybody to inspect it. Some guides are very emphatic that akashic records are closely guarded and information can only be reached by those entitled to it. There is a warning here for mediums who are too free in producing this sort of material.

How many lives is one likely to have and how frequently is one likely to re-incarnate? There does not seem to be any set rule. Different people surely need a different number according to the use made of opportunities. One guide has said that an average person might perhaps have fifty lives.

It is logical to think reincarnation will sometimes be in the male sex and sometimes as a female. Indeed much modern psychological insight regards humans as bisexual in nature. Recent sex changes at the physical level certainly lend support to this. We have all met persons, the masculine woman and the feminine man, who strike us as very possibly having previously had a body – and mind and feelings too – of the opposite sex. Quite apart from this, without the opportunity to live in both modes,

experience would be very incomplete and would steadily become more so.

> We would suggest to you that you look for the male in the female and the female in the male . . . We change our sex many times.[1]

There is much teaching too that we come back in groups. On a large scale, Rudolf Steiner taught that many are now recapitulating the ancient Egyptian period, working upon the same lessons at a slightly higher spiritual spiral, and thus advancing the process of evolution. On a more personal scale many are likely to meet again their peers of old, have common tasks to share with them and old commitments to encounter once more.

Since much of the purpose in reincarnation is to enable formerly unfinished business to be completed, reincarnation accounts, if of value, are bound to include faults and failures. There would be little point in providing material for the pupil to preen himself. It can be objected that we ought to find out for ourselves what is needed, that it should not be handed to one by one's teacher on a plate. Maybe, but in any event one has to do the eating oneself. This is why a causal element is always to be looked for.

Sources of Quotations

1 A private teaching

CHAPTER SEVEN

REINCARNATION: AN EXAMPLE

1

INEVITABLY IT WILL be said: 'If we are to believe in reincarnation, give us an example of what can be usefully told'. This I will endeavour to do by summarising what has been offered of earlier lives of my own which, whether true or false, was produced spontaneously, and *not* at specific request. Necessarily no claim is made that the main threads of these incarnations are entirely correct. Indeed in the main series the teacher insisted that the medium's own mind had introduced some errors which could not be avoided. Inspite of this, strong causal threads can very clearly be seen. They form the plot which brings the narrative into shape.

The stories have been given from two sources. The main source deals with the harsher factors in my past. The second, from a different teacher, is more concerned on the whole with gentler, more inward factors.

From the first source, the sensitive clairaudiently described, over ten sessions, a number of these lives. Then her teacher in trance drew out three main threads in the stories. These have been interwoven over many lives. The first thread is that of the loner, out of step with all around. The second thread is a love for beauty, a search

for the best in everything. The third thread is one of constant rebellion.

The earliest life described was a very ancient one, yet it sets the tone for problems even now not yet resolved in spite of many intervening lives. This was an Incan life where I was described as a woman in a powerful position, this being one of the few civilisations where women have been allowed to hold a high place. My character was arrogant and tyrannical yet I hid beneath this a femininity tormented by a hunger for love and protection inspite of the aggression which hid and prevented it. It was an early life as a loner. After death I was humiliated to find that spiritually I had not done anything like as well as I had supposed. In the following life I passed from this arrogance to its opposite. I became a nomad almost without an identity, rather like a modern drop-out. This can be best represented as a long-term spiritual sulking based on my disappointment. Another early life lay in China, with a position of responsibility once more, but on a more local scale. I now cared deeply about my task. I became a great follower of religious ideas and a disciplinarian; to me it was almost blasphemous to question these. As a result, and through a lack of wisdom I over-protected those in my charge; this only curtailed their individual expansion. It is clear there have been a number of lives where to one degree or another I have had problems with authority, sometimes by over-assertion, sometimes by over-submission, sometimes by denial or rebellion. This Chinese life was one where as can obviously be expected people fawned upon me because of my position. This was the more unpleasant through a degree of insight into such people's real motives. In turn I felt a need for an inner sanctum where both aestheticism and seclusion could act as a balm. This battle between the hurly-burly of responsibility and the

need for seclusion affected my health. This was followed in turn by a peaceful life as a hermit in a pastoral setting. This seems a kind of aftermath life in which inherited love of inner stillness was largely undisturbed. Even today there is still a need to bring inner and outer sides into harmony with one another.

The loner thread was very present in a further ancient life, this time in Egypt, as a priest; here I fell into an arrogant disregard for what was considered proper for my position; I was, too, entirely out of step with the spiritual needs of those in the peasant life around me. In that life I was a really bad lot, disobeying even my own superiors. This was a very wilful loner. In a later life as a monk the loner side took a different form, where my inner withdrawal left me isolated, concerned only with my own spiritual needs. In several more lives I would seek to be a scribe, a recorder, a financial administrator for a monastery, but without any sort of social warmth. Gradually in these lives, it seems that opposite qualities began to be balanced out, the marrying of conventional duties with individuality, and as a result the beginnings of some degree of spiritual freedom. One of these balancing lives was as a student, delicate and fastidious, a university type who loved learning for learning's sake. The lonership then took on a different phase in a European life of the 18th century as a doctor who, though he cared much about helping his patients, was very rude and intolerant to those who, in his view, did not have the sense to look after themselves properly. Fellow doctors would at that time compromise with their patients, but I would not, and left mine in no doubt of my personal views. Because I was too frank this of course led to further isolation.

Now for the second thread, that of a love of beauty and a search for the best in everything. This thread was present in several of the loner lives, and it also reaches

very deeply into my present self. In that disgraceful life in Egypt I would engage the finest artist, and was able easily to recognise a second-rate one. Then I reacted violently against him because I cared so much about beauty. In the much later student life I had a longing to discover the real originators, the prime producers of beauty. This was a very sensitive life, not that of an angry person but one saddened when seeing distortions from true beauty. It was a rather negative period, life in a pastel shade.

In another life as a monk I was one who sought for what I conceived to be highest and best, but in the false terms of paying rapt attention to my religious Supervisor. I had little time for the lower orders. There was conflict because part of me pandered to an importance in my situation which I was not willing to forego. My work at that time was what today would be called the right-hand man to a bishop. I had a mixture of scholarly and perceptive qualities and in the end my superior would take information from me without question because he trusted my ability and judgment. Within such monastic limits I developed also a certain degree of business acumen and was certainly not above arguing and bargaining, nor was I free from abusing my position at times. It could be said that whilst I still desired the best the result was a considerably tainted use of it. In the later life as the rough-tongued doctor, where my temperament made me into a solitary, this produed a drab emotional life. My love of the best showed itself in the refusal, already mentioned, to compromise at all. The best I saw as what was best in terms of the patient's needs; I would certainly fight to save a patient's life. In another sense I cared for the best in that I was intolerant of all the medical abuses of the day.

The third thread of rebellion has run through many lives and is also an important one. In the life of the priest

in ancient Egypt this was strong in my flamboyant refusal to conform. I would allow no intrusion on my choices. This brought about an inverted hunger and pain which led me to make people suffer in turn. Ritual and ceremony was demanded in those times against which again I rebelled. In the later life of a student, where I tended to retire from the demands of life, this cushioned me against the violence of the times, and my diligence also protected me. Nevertheless it was a life of taking the line of least resistance, rather like the man with one talent who buried it. The opting out was a kind of pale rebellion. In the monastic life as assistant to the bishop there came about a dominant and colourful incarnation; because of my position as right-hand man I was a target for corruption. However, I resisted this and was very stable, but there were certain battles with conscience. There was also inner conflict because whilst I would try to conform to ordinary codes of monastic daily life my heart was not there. A temptation came to win advancement at the cost of abandoning certain moral values which, for me, were important. I refused this advancement and this has stood me in good stead since.

As the doctor, the rebellious thread showed because I would not conform to expected patterns, though I longed to be liked. Being rebellious showed itself also in bad manners. In that life too I would have nothing at all to do with God or religion.

Turning now to the set of incarnations which were described briefly over the years by my guide Peter, these relate only to lives that I have shared with him. Most of these are concerned with more kindly and inward aspects of character. But the life of which he spoke most sadly and sternly was set in a monastery at the time of the Spanish Inquisition. We meant well, he said, but it was a sorry life. Although Peter did not say so, it is from here

that I believe I derive an aspect of character which relates to the role of devil's advocate. Thinking, talking or writing today tends to become obscured by a tangle and complication of contrary aspects which confuse or make weaker the real point intended. Whether the source is correctly attributed or not the presence of this aspect cannot be doubted. It has often reduced me to ineffectiveness of presentation when it was quite unnecessary for this to happen.

There was also a life as monks together at Assisi.

> In the Franciscan life we were learning spiritual truths, and we learned to care. We had been taught to appreciate beauty, taught to be part of ritual, and then in that life in Italy we learned to care in depth, and although we studied many books, it was the discipline of the self that we learned there, to control it and to be able to reach out to God and not to expect God automatically to come to us.[1]

The flaw was, as Peter said, that each really wanted spiritual reward for himself. Then there was a life as a woman who had to learn the lesson that physical beauty fades and that it is not enough; the need instead is for beauty of soul. Peter was my servant which seems very strange to me. He tells of his joy then in watching me learn something of that particular lesson. On a more cheerful note there was a shared life at Glastonbury before the dissolution of the monasteries. Today to wander in the Abbey grounds is for me like coming home. It is the easiest of places for making direct contact with Peter, and equally easy in which to meditate.

What then of the future, with this burden of failures, forceful or gentle, to carry from the past? It will be asked whether these stories are of any practical value today. First, they show how deep are some of the roots of

character defects; second, the medium's trance teacher proposed some practical working tools, which if used well would strengthen my present temperament and redress its balance. If I were able, he said, to find a degree of peace with the God-force then I would be able to overcome the rebellious factor which in past lives has so often robbed me of serenity of mind. My sense of beauty and perfection would come to my aid, through recognition of it in countless situations. As a loner I could develop a fuller cognisance of the various needs which other people have in themselves, but which it would be impossible for me to recognise until I was ready to acknowledge and serve the same needs in myself. Thus lonership could grow into companionship.

These threads have been put into my hands by loving help from discarnate teachers. It is not at all difficult unfortunately to recognise in my present nature the continuing legacy of these threads. My own insightful memory was not strong enough to arouse these past lives into consciousness. Therefore it was found necessary to help by showing where these present threads had their original source. This produced valuable clues as to how best to deal with their true aims. This I would not have had without their help. Naturally I am very grateful for it.

Looking back at the links between these lives it is very clear that like many people I have been a prodigal son, so often wasting moral assets and constantly falling into debased choices of values. Each is bound to bear within him the wounds of his own unresolved failures. Every item has of course to be repaired. I can honestly say that each one of these threads relates to faults in my present character. This to me gives indisputable proof of the causality within the narrative. The remedy continues to lie in my own hands.

2

When examining reincarnational causality as spiritual fact, it is easy at first to suppose that one proceeds from imperfect qualities to better and better expressions of the same qualities. It is far from working out in so simple a way. Thus one life, or part of one life, may seem to show a less advanced level than that of a former life. This becomes less of a riddle if, as guides teach, only one part, perhaps quite a small part of the total being comes into any one incarnation, a part where concentrated attention is urgently needed to put it right. A subsequent incarnation could be similarly directed to facets other than those now being attended to. Reincarnation needs to be looked on as a carpet woven of many threads, now one section and then another taking it in turn to fill the foreground. But the carpet has an overall design, and causality shows a repetition of various parts of the pattern, until all is made complete. What has been earned, or where failure has been in former lives, may not all appear in the present life. It may not be locally relevant. Its turn will come about later. It will return to face one until the rough-hewn ashlar has been re-cut, polished into its true intended shape. Hence the need for patience and compassion both towards oneself and in observing the lacks in others.

There is also the changing of the curriculum for a while. Within the course of a life we find ourselves acting at times, we hardly know why, in a quite different manner than would have seemed both appropriate and easy in earlier years. Particularly is this likely to happen when the target turns into a more difficult one, and when real effort needs to be made to tune up a former quality into higher levels. Increased spiritual energy undoubtedly has another effect; it stirs up the lower side in oneself, makes

100

it angry so to speak, and so another fight is started within. One learns to be patient with oneself when old lessons, previously considered learned, turn up and need to be worked at yet again.

Certain lives too represent a swing of the pendulum. When things have gone too far in a former life, in the following incarnation we may have a horror of the very thing willingly embraced before. A guide once told a story – he did not name Richard III nor was he making a historical statement – he was just taking a picture familiar to all. Using this fictional device the guide spoke of one who had brought about the murder of two young boys who might later have disadvantaged him. The story went on that in a later life this man was very gentle and peaceful, with a great horror of violence. He had two sons who were the apple of his eye. Skating on a wintry day, the two sons fell through the ice and were drowned. Few events in real life are likely to reproduce in opposite shape a former event in so obvious a way but the principle is clear. As Buddhist teaching says, if you wish to know about your former lives, examine the circumstances which surround you now. This father's gentleness of character made his contemporaries say that he was a man ahead of his time. The guide in telling the story, said that really he was behindhand. He had the task of learning qualities at double the speed as it were, to make up for time lost before. So appearances can be very deceptive. For this as well as for deeper reasons it is important to avoid condemning one's contemporaries for their lack of certain qualities. They may have had them in excess before. We certainly know very little of what is written on another's scroll of life. There are missing chapters we cannot see. We cannot be our brother's keeper. We simply do not know enough about him.

The central factor behind reincarnation is how progress

can best be made in refining the character and making of it a better vehicle. A frequent precept, given by spiritual teachers of many faiths, is that it is wise to work towards the golden mean. Blake, speaking in his direct way, said: 'Let the fool persist in his folly and he will become a wise man'. In one trance teacher's words, an excess of error gradually becomes melted down, as it were, and moderated in subsequent lives until it eventually takes on its true shape, and then becomes a positive quality, part of one's spiritual light. It takes time for this melting down process to come about; the same teacher, in another image, says it is most often brought about by those abrasive qualities in life, which none of us escape on earth.

I must conclude this short account with the legacies the teacher says are still amongst my handicaps. A danger of being bigoted, too willing to denigrate other's beliefs. There is still the former tendency to seclusion, creating a stumbling block where one is unable to be one of the crowd, when one is even out of step with one's peers, and too often with the society in which born. There has still been a marked tendency to rebel: against my former religion, against my professional training, against my Masonic instruction, against my social environment. A degree of spiritual freedom has been won, however, found as in earlier lives from within myself and from nature. I find my worship of God is directed as though to a distant force; I find it hard to accept God in terms of compassionate love for even myself. This makes for a less happy and companionable incarnation. Then there is, still to reckon with, the indolent streak from being a nomad, the tendency to prefer to be a nonentity, to sink into the background and to bypass challenges. It remains more comfortable in a wrong way to bring about such a deliberate self-effacement.

102

How are such tiresome defects best seen? If material from former lives comes one's way either in a narrative of this kind, or from occasional unexpected shafts of intuition at deeply attuned moments, or else by uncomfortable prickings of conscience, the true response is to tune oneself to one's inner spiritual note wherever one can come to recognise it. The deep can overcome the shallow. Certainly willingness of response is needed and the subsequent hard spiritual work it always points to. Else old habits from the past become even more ingrown. Spiritual insights can be expected to provide a dusty answer when one applies them to personality matters. It is however important to cultivate detachment about one's failures. Detachment is far from being indifference. It is best to give up self-blame with its egotistic overtones, to shrug one's shoulders, to resolve to try harder today, next month and in the next incarnation; to tell one's truth to oneself and in place of self-justification be willing to accept self-forgiveness.

3

It has not been my purpose to proclaim this fragmentary story of a chain of incarnations as established fact. The information is particular and not general, and, as is obvious, it is impossible to prove. How far the story holds together, how strong its internal coherence, is a matter of opinion for the onlooker. The sceptic is welcome to his doubtless negative opinion. He can look at the causality which to me so clearly exists between one episode and the next, and say that the whole is no more than an example of 'jobbing backwards', that acquaintance with my present character is simply re-told as fanciful episodes from a totally unknown and probably imaginary past. He

can explain all away, except the light which the stories first brought to me concerning my present situation and opportunities. That is their real point.

The sceptic leaves me unperturbed since I am the one who can best *experience* the causality, as distinct from judging it, the only one who can say how the events – and they are mostly ones of little credit or of downright failure – fit my present struggles and difficulties of temperament as the glove fits the hand. The causality brings a need to overcome or improve characteristics in a way I find urgent. During the seven or eight years since the narrative reached me, its precision of causality has not diminished at all. As a result I have, I hope, gained a little both in decision and in integrity. The causality has thus proved itself valid, to me at least, by its work upon my character. For friends who have had the opportunity of receiving a narrative from the same source, the causality indicated has been quite different, strongly individual and with no mere easy duplications.

Because my own narrative reflects so little credit upon me, and points so clearly to 'unfinished business', is precisely why its impact has been so convincing. It is alas not at all the story I would have wished to tell.

Sources of Quotations

1   A private teaching

CHAPTER EIGHT

A GLIMPSE INTO THE GROUP SOUL

1

NEW INNER VALUES, as they come to be sensed, also need expression on earth, or partially at least. A part of the inner man after all exists on earth as well as the outer man, but, as Gurdjieff and Ouspensky said in their various ways, the inner man is largely asleep. An important purpose of the discarnate guide, whose own inner self is awake, is to awaken it also in his pupil. So in providing an enlarged picture, the guide is also making a call to action.

He may choose to introduce in a preliminary way the concept of a group soul. The direction of discarnate teaching is that we are far from being the single self with which we are apparently identified. What of other beings, teachers, peers, companions of our being? Single bliss is inconceivable in any generous future pattern of living. Hence a further spiritual out-working awaits us which teachers speak of as rejoining the group soul to which one belongs. Within a group soul, members are not like soldiers, whose task alone unites them, and in whom the residue of their character has comparatively little to do with the main task ahead. In ways both intimate and mysterious, it is more like a closely-linked family, who

know each other's particular qualities exceptionally well because there is a common substance within them all. Again like a family, the group exists over very many generations.

The main aspect of the group soul to be considered here – and it is only one of a number of aspects – is limited to the earthly end of what essentially is a very intimate partnership, best seen as an allegiance with caring beings 'out there'. These caring beings invite us to work alongside themselves as a member of a team in bettering one aspect or another of earth life.

One cannot be said to gravitate towards a particular group soul; in some part of one's being one already is, or is not, a member of it. Thus one cannot 'join' it; one can only recognise it. This comes about through a spontaneous desire arising from within the heart to work for certain ideals. The invitation will come, usually from behind the scenes, from one of these teachers, whose full closeness is unlikely to be known. The invitation is always to work, but never to work for private reward. That would be a contradiction in terms. In time the individual comes to recognise that his real identity lies in being a fragment within a much larger whole.

At first this may well be rejected, partly because of its unfamiliarity. This is reinforced by the reluctance of the natural man to what he first looks on as a call to abandon his present familiar self, and the overlordship of it which he takes to be his birthright. For this reason a group soul concept at first is often far from welcome.

2

How can one grow into acceptance of a group soul? The very meaning of the word 'individual' is 'undivided' thus

implying one is interiorly linked with the God-force and also with one's fellow beings. It is selfishness which tells one otherwise. The saint differs from the sinner because his family is not local, but the whole world. Being a loner is a strange limitation, born, like all other relationship variations from a strand laid hold of in earlier lives and reinforced in later incarnations until at last strength comes to reverse it. Meanwhile the loner, like the man of family life, finds both a gain and a limitation through his choice. Somewhere in the present situation the right thread lies hidden which can lead on to something larger. Earthly brotherhood, for instance, is much more than do-gooding, for too often that too includes a selfish element – as the robust and healthy judgment of everyday human nature has a speedy way of recognising. Brotherhood lies in the joy of seeing into the heart of the brother who needs help. There is no wish to make the brother like oneself – a doubtful compliment anyhow. The wish is to help the brother to be himself.

Men and women derive a strength from working together. Society, the religious orders, the regiment, the charitable association, even the committee and the board-room, all gain through united force when harmony prevails within. In the inner worlds the same principle of companionship applies and in greater depth, through having its roots in spiritual nourishment.

Links of love and obligation exist between all those in a long-term spiritual group. The group has been ensouled with a long term spiritual task unique to it, and the ensoulment comes from a spiritual leader in whose being the purpose and need of the group first became lodged. In one aspect the leader is the spiritual father, the members his spiritual family, even when in a local sense placed in quite different earth families spread perhaps over many countries and over a long span of time.

The task of the group can be envisaged as a basic ideal, first seen by the spiritual leader as a shimmering light-filled reality for the future and then moving gradually downwards and outwards, as its members seek to see and fulfill it in stumbling earth terms. Within the chain of incarnations its members work step by step, individually and in partnerships to bring about particular aspects of the whole long term purpose of the group. Companions in the group will come close, recognised or unrecognised, sometimes in partnership and sometimes in seeming opposition, thereby perhaps teaching one another the better. The whole story needs a long perspective, for the full tale to be told can be expected to be a glorious one. Whether recognised or not, the group as a whole is inwardly urging each member onward to continue his corner of the struggle; sometimes in a way he cannot account for in himself, nor can he wholly explain the emptiness which can come to him if he gives up, and loses himself in the routine gratifications of daily living. To give up is one of the commonest human tragedies.

3

The idea of a group, however imperfectly glimpsed, needs to be never allowed to become diminished into something minor and unimportant. It must not be made into a refuge, for instance, at times when it is proving hard to face up to earth difficulties. Nor must it ever be thought of as some elitist clique. The glamour readily pinned on to it needs to be changed into a recognition that what is involved in long-term membership includes much that is at present very imperfect.

It is sometimes useful to look on the prospect of growing into this group soul more closely after death, as

part of what Lawrence Hyde named the planes of ascension. But since human nature remains so imperfect, planes of return and of regeneration as well as planes of ascension are required. Aspects of regeneration are plentifully implied in the reincarnation account in the last chapter. Within a group soul, in terms of ascension one can look forward, though not on earth, to a rejoining, a home-coming, a surrender to a larger task seen fully only by the ultimate group soul leader, and a very gradual blissful absorption into it.

Meanwhile we certainly cannot see into the assembled group soul because it would be too bright for us to bear. Even a reflected light can be too bright. The light, so often spoken of in discarnate accounts in which a senior is clothed, and in which he becomes lost to our vision, is a fragment of Shelley's white light of eternity and it is we, in simply being our earth self, who stain its white radiance. Poets, telling sometimes more than they consciously know, reflect truly the unseen as well as the seen. Shelley conjured up no fanciful picture.

The group soul is best considered as existing together at multiple levels. Senior and junior members participate, though a concept of lesser and greater relates to present aspect and achievement and not to essential being.

Some perhaps all the same feel overwhelmed at the prospect of so enhanced a life as the group soul offers. They find they can orientate themselves better to their immediate problems, with the help of their own conscience. In this way they feel more at home. Others prefer a more generalised picture, without touching the especial intimacy characterising the group soul concept. Enough that they feel a grand alliance which each strengthens through his own work. This is an aspect of the communion of souls. As part of the mystery of the distant horizon, the group soul whispers to us that we belong to

the universe in a deeply intimate way, and that seemingly hostile factors in life cannot in the end dispel this hope. This is one antidote to the view that we live in an alien mechanistic universe. Experience pointing to the more intimate view is necessarily not easy to come by. In the group soul there lies a deep aspect of true human belonging together, life no longer as a battle but as companionship.

4

On earth a spiritual organisation can arise which draws within it some who are already inwardly members of the group whose ideals and purposes the earth portion fragmentarily represents. Every such group has its own spiritual uniqueness.

On earth a strange yet unmistakable incompleteness is sensed, as if each knows there is a part of himself from which he is somehow mysteriously separated. This belongs to the human condition. Yet the limitation and the yearning felt so painfully can be pointing all the while towards the very thing from which one meanwhile feels so exiled. Some of these indications are fragmentary and elusive. That is why the group soul concept is only very gradually being introduced into the general corpus of discarnate teaching, as a life-enhancing area at present largely an area of preparation. It provides an exercise in inner self-discrimination, and more important it offers a wonderful warmth of generosity of which the earth members are only a few of the recipients. It is life more abundant. This is part of the larger house of being on inner planes. On earth, there can be no more than minor reflections of it, adumbrations.

One idea which theology presents is that of a church as

custodian of a divine authority to which it calls for absolute adherence; an extreme example is fundamentalist Christianity. In the group soul, as sensed at present, this concept of a church as a guardian body is replaced by something a little more akin to the Catholic idea of a church invisible.

It would seem that in the inner world, there is the constant presence of powerful spiritual ideas of an archetypal kind, which then gradually penetrates into the minds of high beings there. Then in turn, with their help, something of this essence becomes dimly felt within the mental and emotional climate of the age, glimpsed and then partly absorbed and expressed according to limited human insights.

In such a climate any idea of future punishment for refusing to follow one particular creed becomes simplistic as well as cruel. Irrespective of creeds and congregations, small groups are likely to come together to explore aspects of these ideas felt to be of particular significance to them, groups happy and interested in living alongside differently oriented groups in terms of friendship and mutual interest and not in the least as rival missions.

What will the true human unit ultimately be found to be? Will it be the individual? Or the twin soul? This is a very elusive and often over-romanticised concept, and really belongs to something much deeper than a harmony between personal man and personal woman. Teachers talk of it seldom and with caution.

Or will the true unit be the group soul? That a group soul exists to which in the best part of ourselves we already belong brings a deep feeling of reassurance of one's destiny. Much of its strength lies in the very fact that it welds the individual into his particular place in a true brotherhood. By definition members of a group soul reach a fuller realisation through companionship in a

111

common task, in the deep purpose which steadily pervades and so to speak overcomes the lesser parts of its members by transforming them into its own reality. By a process of private tuning-in to the innermost parts of one's self on earth, something which can best be described as a sacred harmony within this soul brotherhood comes to be felt. It brings to the individual an inner strengthening for his particular work.

Nevertheless the actual expression on earth of group soul work will often be lessened – in a very necessary way – through inevitable human limitations, by which its wings will be clipped. It needs must fly close to the ground.

When Baden-Powell founded the Boy Scout movement, it can be expected that the primary purposes were conceived and debated within his group soul in the inner worlds and that he was probably assisted by other members of the group, incarnated like him to give it impulse on earth. Later with its earth growth a great many people will have given allegiance to the movement without being members of the group soul. The archetypal idea is likely to have come from the group, but Baden-Powell, however important his work, may have been a much smaller part of his movement than we usually suppose.

Towards the end of the 19th century a Christian Minister, the Rev. Stainton Moses, as has been said earlier, found himself engaged in theological arguments through the process then called automatic writing. The writing was dissociated enough to allow him to read a book on another subject whilst it was being produced. It attempted to free his conscience from old orthodoxy and win acceptance of a much wider picture. The argument took place (unless one prefers to say that all along Stainton Moses was only arguing with himself) with a communicator who called himself Imperator. (Incidentally

112

quite a deal of the flavour of this being comes over.) Forty years or so later Imperator made another appearance in a well established private group where some forty or fifty people of different social levels met regularly in an effort of constructive prayer to improve world conditions. Imperator said an interesting thing; that he saw well the possibilities of such a group, but that if he found this one was not becoming fully welded together spiritually he would withdraw. In point of fact, he did withdraw after a few months, and two or three years later, for other reasons, the group was disbanded. Yet some of its members may have belonged together in a group soul.

As another medium has more recently described it, discarnate beings are interested in creating an integrated structure, a Gestalt, the purpose of which depends upon its members working for a larger scheme than any of them can express individually. She described a group of five discarnate persons, some of them psychical researchers and all known to me by name or in person. (Their names were only given at the close of the half-dozen sessions involved.) The medium described how she faced a necessity new to her in listening to a voice which seemed to her to belong to no one of these five but was a composite and impersonal one, but for which each of the members were needed. This was a difficult and pioneering feat of mediumship. To show the possibilities was perhaps more important than what was actually said. This could be a true glimpse intended to show in one way how a group soul can work on a particular project. It will be of great interest to watch if future attempts come about which can be seen clearly to relate deeply and certainly to such impersonal though closely-linked activity.

It may be too, and experience suggests it, that if a number of humans are incarnated on earth together to help to bring about some fraction of the total task of their

group it is not likely that they have incarnated together for the first time. There may have been in the past many interwoven relationships between them, but it may be much the best for present purposes that these remain locked away. An especially large squeeze of the anaesthetising sponge of the waters of Lethe applied at birth, could mercifully obscure some of the personal emotional abysses and entanglements otherwise likely to arise again, and make the group work impossible to be carried out.

Some work on earth will be a very preliminary preparation for true soul group work. It foreshadows it. It can cluster around a discarnate teacher, known only in the limited way in which the trance presents him, whether as an Egyptian priest or an ancient Chinese philosopher, or in whatever guise. Members of such groups can work faithfully together over the years in united service – and here those anaesthetic waters may be at work – though feeling surprisingly little in terms of personal attachments to one another. They come together, carry on their task, largely in silence, and depart again with the minimum of personal ado, and surely this is for the betterment of the work. This can be the form needed to be taken by many groups. We know so little of the depths and intertwinings which underlie even some of our most seemingly casual earth contacts. It is certain that we know even less of what lies behind deeper ones.

Taking part in such group work, at however simple a level, is not to be undertaken lightly. It is an apprenticeship which later will involve processes of both loss and surrender within the self. On the spiritual path a loss however painful is always later found to have been also a gain, perhaps of a very unexpected kind. The loss can however never be made in order to secure the gain; else there would be no surrender of the self. An

intellectual can complain that in this world of inner allegiances one is offered a seemingly tangled logic; that one is most oneself when not oneself, but a part of a larger unity. He can complain that it is like saying that a son is only truly himself because he is part of his father. Nevertheless the innermost leader of a group soul can be said to have imparted, as a gift of love, something of his own spiritual substance to every member of the group, and it is in this sense that each is indeed a son or daughter.

In the group soul, 'part' has a wider meaning, both grander and yet also more intimate. For the leader of the group soul, of whom individually one is thus spiritually a part, creates the purpose and destiny of the group. In battle the subordinate may seriously doubt the wisdom of the orders given to him, but he carries them out and perhaps dies in doing so. In the group the wisdom is unquestionable. It forms the bliss of the relationship. It is very hard to express its quality. It may even be that in the end the combined wisdom of the group will become wider than that of the leader, who first gave of his own wisdom to it. In a relationship of love, no weighing of giving and receiving can come about, since each of these is part of the loving. A line from Epipsychidion, though within a quite different context, expresses something of the spirit of the group soul when it declares that 'Between unequals, equal love is sweet'. The real problem in trying to apprehend something of the group soul is the near impossibility of overcoming the idea of personal relationship, since in the group soul normal human ways of feeling work towards a sense of unity which in its fullness altogether exceeds our present understanding, but which it is promised by the leader will in the end be found exquisitely satisfying.

There is however as always another human aspect which attaches itself to it and degrades it. To desire to

have this satisfaction before one is ready to undergo the disciplines and the abandonment needed to reach it, is merely to fall into emotional greed. And that sentiment certainly does not belong to the group soul.

For entry into this world of inner allegiance can never be forced. True allegiances come about through their interior reality, and the personal element, as in monastic disciplines, will always be subdued to the impersonal.

The harmony to be aimed at is therefore a sacred one, a living at a depth which relates more fully to a later part of our existence but which, in small part, is already in our possession now. It takes a very long while to learn to live, even for a few precious moments, in unfamiliar rooms in the spacious house which is our real self.

CHAPTER NINE

SOME PARAMETERS

1

IN THE WIDE process of growing towards the oneness of all life, the appearance of teachers from the discarnate world forms a part, but it still remains that earth life itself is the real instructor. Yet discarnate help is also part of that experience. Clearly it must not be allowed – as indeed it no way wishes – to supplant the direct impact of earth experience. Its aim is to enrich that experience and add help to it consciously, as well as in our inner being or during the sleep state from which it only gradually wells up into consciousness.

In their direct contribution, guides present this inner material, however complex, in essentially simple terms. This is a long way from the intellectual complexity the human mind so often prefers. Its simplicity, residing in the teacher's own vision, reveals what so often complexity hides. Love for other beings, personal and impersonal, remains the best route towards the recognition and overcoming of the barriers to the inner life. This implies a generosity of being towards life and towards others living it.

In the same way, to be open in disclosing one's own shadow, which each carries around, stirs others to

approach and face their own shadow area in turn. To acknowledge the shadow for what it is, is also to begin to defeat its powers. Insight leads to action. As the occult saying puts it, energy follows thought. Recognition is the first part of action, sometimes more difficult than action, sometimes less so.

The guide helps to resolve this private drama both through direct insight and by presenting for his student's help some part of the Ageless Wisdom, so that he can then bring it into play in daily modern living. To encourage the pupil in his use of the Ageless Wisdom is to encourage him to enlarge himself.

Spiritual teaching aims then to offer parameters, though necessarily still incomplete, within which earth life can be lived a little more widely, with greater intention, and more in tune with a great purpose behind all. Those who founded or fostered the world religions demonstrated this in practice through living a nearly perfect life on earth. The cream of their disciples followed the same path as far as they were able. It proves to be always a path of sacrifice.

The immediate path offered by discarnate guides and teachers and geared to modern life is not so severe. It seems indeed so much easier at first that some mistake it for self-indulgence and then of course miss its direction. Others are reluctant to accept it for a variety of reasons; they fear its source, or they do not care for it if a guide says: 'We now wish to teach you what you believe you already know'. Or they attempt to rely upon their own prowess, allowing no teacher's words to come really close to them.

If the help of guides does come to be accepted, they gradually show us as much of ourselves as we can bear. The most important obstacles, the deeper part of the shadow, are the result of deeds and omissions from

former lives. Guides do not ram these down our throat; they help us gently to work upon seeing and then overcoming them and thus avoiding the compounding effect which results if they are continued as formerly. Besides obstacles within and without, there are signposts, 'wayshowings' which they present at a decisive moment on the road. At other times, like Hamlet's father, guides need to whet our well-nigh blunted purpose. They hope not to need to.

The parameters offered, relevant to the present time, are framed so as not to distract attention from the main task of self-regeneration. They sometimes include items of what may be called pre-history, for which objective evidence is obviously unavailable. (The rationalist here can produce a short sharp laugh; others however come in time to think the joke is on him.) Purposeful glimpses are given of occult laws at work, and of the functioning of other kingdoms of beings on earth. At the same time Chinese walls are shown beyond which it is not profitable to try to penetrate. It must not be supposed in the least however, that what guides thus offer with one hand they take away with the other. The way into deeper parts of these realms always remains open, but the qualification needed is growth. Then the parameters widen. The help is there, the vision is described, the readiness must be in the pupil.

Where then do these parameters lie? In order to become aware – as guides are found to be aware – of a divine force at work behind every natural and mortal scene, guides first invite men and women to become open to an inner recognition of moral laws at work. Reincarnational laws are one particular example. The meanings found do not lie in logical persuasion, but by direct impact upon a pupil's own nature. When the moments of vision come, each begins to find there are

parts of himself which he must begin to prepare to leave behind. The encrustations of the material world need to start to drop away. Men do not like to abandon familiar and fixed values, so various refusals of acceptance come about. The superior insights of teachers, thanks to their love for their pupil, see what is immediately possible for him. This is part of the meaning of the well-known saying that when the pupil is ready, the master appears. Before this the guide, or his deputy, will have been at work behind the scenes, looking for where he can begin to break through the defences behind which the student has for long entrenched himself. The process of breaking through is not one of intrusive assault. The pupil, not the teacher, is the one who is usually sure he knows best. The teacher watches for early stirrings in the pupil's sleep. As he stirs, the teacher's words may not at first seem very significant. They are likely to be quiet in their impact. They wait for the pupil's understanding to awaken.

Seen on a wider screen the way takes a very long time to traverse, alike for the individual and for mankind in general. The fragments of pre-history, which the teacher chooses to hint at, speak of long-ceased civilisations in no terms of glamour but rather with regret for what was won but then lost again, as power became used for selfish aims. That is no unfamiliar story.

Pre-history (or if one prefers it, occult teaching) goes on to say, through various different sources, that at regular intervals a fresh spiritual impulse is brought for mankind to recognise and work for until this impulse wanes and is then in turn replaced by another. These take place around every two thousand years. They are reflected in astrological lore. Thus the Piscean age now ending brought the impulse through which the mystical and self-surrendering spiritual aspects in mankind could develop active qualities expressed by Jesus, its leader and

exemplar. The next impulse, that of the forthcoming Aquarian age, is now beginning to come into expression. An Aquarian examplar is likely, whether in the form of man or woman, or indirectly through illumination reaching down into the interior being. It is expected to bring about a much truer balance between masculine and feminine qualities. Yet as the Bible foretells of such times, false prophets inevitably appear too. Already a leader's appearance has been confidently prophesied for a date now in the past. Prophets of limited stature, or with feet of clay, show themselves in the end for what they are. It is not to be assumed that the Piscean age will disappear overnight and be replaced next day by the Aquarian; it is likely to take the form of a gradual overlapping, a waning and waxing over a couple of hundred years or so.

Hence at so important an epoch, facing both a possibility of planetary destruction, and the gradual permeation of a new spiritual impetus, it would be surprising indeed if there were not an intensive effort on the part of spiritual teachers to help bring about the birth of the new age in as harmonious and fruitful way as possible. The Aquarian age is declared to be one of penetration of the mind by the spirit, bringing achievements through spiritual perceptions, or else betrayal by choosing destructive use of rational Frankenstein-like achievements. The developing of the new spiritual insights suited to the age will perhaps need much fuller creative use of leisure. This may be an important task. Much will depend as always on the qualities in man himself.

2

Obligation therefore rests upon the guide to work with each pupil at his present level of need. This duty appears

to be a sacred one. When asked for bread the guide cannot by spiritual law offer a stone. The whole texture of the work of the teacher forms part of the moral realm, as he attempts to show that the spiritual essence within each pupil expresses and is part of the law by which the whole of creation acts out its purpose. The more a man relates himself to this, it follows that the more truly he is *becoming himself*. All, including himself, his peers, his teachers, are part of the law itself because created by the same God force.

Deep within the heart of every man and woman lies an ever-burning longing for his true home. The truth lies more in the longing, than in the immediate representations believed to show its likeness. Some men's pictures of heaven are intensely boring to others. Home can only come about when man has fully given himself to, and lost himself in, spiritual law. This after all is the first of the two laws of which Jesus spoke: to love God with all one's heart and mind and strength. And as man comes to recognise that all men and women partake in the spiritual law so the second law of Jesus comes into effect; to love one's neighbour as oneself.

Discarnate teachers all point to these two laws in various ways. These teachers, of course, as indeed they hasten both to say and to mean, are in no way perfect. They differ in emphasis from one another. They most earnestly say that their knowledge of the spiritual is far from complete. At key moments they withdraw and seek instructions from those above them, to whom their own work is joyfully obedient.

'Going home' is often seen in a local interpretation as casting off the shackles of earth and finding one's ease in the Summerland. Other meanings are deeper. It is a very important part of homecoming to find one's place in the group soul. Another important thread in occult pre-

history is that mankind for thousands of years has gradually entered deeper and deeper into materialism, in order to experience at first hand its limitations and its horrors, in order to face the further task of gradually transforming it into obedience to spiritual law. It is the story of man being cast into a wilderness in order to make it blossom as the rose. In occult teaching the arrival of the Aquarian age marks the beginnings of the return to man's own spiritual source; the deeply significant hour in the cosmic clock when his path is reversed, and he is drawn slowly upwards along every step of the path which he has already travelled downwards, so gradually regaining his real status and wholeness of being. This is indeed a profound 'going home'. It throws a valuable lifeline to the soul exhausted by the present painful part of the long journey.

In his deepest self, man already knows that his true place can only be as part of a whole. This does not stop him falling prey to incomplete opposites. He can be a loner and partake of the essential heresy of the prodigal son, or he can be one who accepts the general judgment, over-valuing it because it is the majority one. Each way has its productive use; but each prefers the near to the far. Each is refusing what must in the end be found: that all are one, and that as the Lady Julian's vision told her, 'All shall be well and all manner of thing shall be well'. But being part of the whole is something very different from being part of the crowd, or from belonging to no kingdom but one's own.

Many present discarnate teachers are members of what is usually known as the Great White Brotherhood. They state that this Brotherhood is very ancient; they name its teaching the Ageless Wisdom. As far as we can know, it claims no one individual as its head; indeed its sources lie completely beyond our reach. A jibe is often made – nor

is it without some justification – that a guide is presented in the form of an Indian, a Chinaman, an Egyptian, a nun, but seldom a plain Englishman. There do appear of course plain Englishmen, and Scots and Irish too, but their role is usually introductory. Perhaps too some of those from far-off races have also incarnated comparatively recently as plain Englishmen, but prefer former lives where they lived in a less contaminated way, closer to spiritual sources, and can from this chosen presentation throw better light upon their pupil's present difficulties. With a White Brotherhood of ancient origin but modern functioning, why should it be objected to if something of a 'League of Nations' is drawn upon? It is not to be denied that a Chinese guide usually reveals in his teaching a patience, a courtesy, and a down-to-earth humorous perception, well-worth listening to. So is the contribution of simple peace and purity brought by a nun. It is a bit stand-offish and peculiarly English, to object to help from sources which are thought to be foreign but are found to be every bit as much at home in the White Brotherhood as the Englishman. One oriental teacher remarked with somewhat British humour, that there is one quality in which the English excel and that is the art of making excuses to delay setting out on the spiritual path.

It would certainly not be appropriate to claim that the Ageless Wisdom forms the main stream behind the great world religions, easy though it is to regard one's own choice as being at the head of the league table. The great world religions and the Ageless Wisdom are likely to have common sources, but all vanish beyond our sight, and beyond that of guides also, if it is attempted to follow them up-stream. Parochialism is a handicap, and all religions come together in the insight of the mystic, whatever his race. Who would say, least of all the mystic, that the vision which has fallen upon him is final truth?

Not even St Francis who was given insight on Alvernia to mysteries which he said were so sacred that he was forbidden to tell of them.

The essential spiritual vision is very simple. That is why as always in the field of morals it is so very difficult to follow, as earnest and saintly Christians have often said.

The holy person of whatever denomination or none is the simplest who, little entangled in the self, finds on that account plenty of time and freedom to know and to love others. The simplicity cannot come about until the complicated obstacles in the self have been removed.

It is odd that guides who show in themselves a considerable degree of simplicity, and often turn complicating questions into simple replies, are usually written off as being platitudinous and obvious, much as in the old story of the wise men who, visiting the aged St John, were told no more than: 'Brethren, love one another'. They replied: 'Yes, yes we know that' and went away disgusted. But the saint's simplicity saw that they did not know it.

It may be questioned, if the solutions to right conduct lie in simplicity, why is it that guides sometimes say they are longing to tell us more but that we are not yet ready for it? Part of the meaning is that there are both heights and depths in humanity which they do not speak about because we should be unable to handle either. To be told of the smallest personal perfection is likely to corrupt by taking attention away from faults as yet undealt with. And depths created by our own past could be such – and guides sometimes say so – that to know of them would crush us, and prove a burden too big to carry. It is hard enough to despair of humanity, to read in history of the unspeakable and useless cruelties perpetrated by men on men; what if we ourselves committed some of the worst or even much lesser ones? If it is too difficult even to give up a few

smokes or drinks, might we not despair altogether if confronted with the wrongs which eventually have to be redressed? The frail self we know on earth could not stand the polar extremes of human behaviour; for the majority it is best to work within a temperate climate. Guides therefore lead us gently along the lower slopes of the spiritual mountain, gauging accurately the gradient we can manage. The pace chosen is not of great concern; since in reality there is no time, then there is all the time in the world. We are given brief glimpses above our station; but each is only fully released to the next step above him on the Jacob's Ladder when he has earned the spiritual muscle even for that short climb. It is alas well known that those who set themselves a lofty and exacting spiritual target are the ones most likely to encounter an early fall. Spiritual ambition is a heady thing. Nonetheless times do arrive when a guide begins to ask more of his charge than before. In an image used by St John of the Cross, the day comes when a mother needs to put both herself and her child away from former caresses. What once gave strength can later become enervating. Most who have tried to follow closely their guide's instruction meet the time when he consciously withdraws for a while, leaving the pupil to strengthen his own muscles, by attempting to rise nearer to his teacher's level of vision instead of expecting the teacher to come down to his own earthly one.

It is part of the pupil's role therefore to develop a sensitising of the inner antennae, a process of expectation that there is more, perhaps already hinted but missed at first. Part of the health of these antennae is that they cannot be stretched through a process of mental pushing. That always leads to misconception, and always has its base in egotism. Antennae work through a patient, relaxed and quietly alert attention.

126

Guides are in a good position to offer a picture of how to live on earth. After all they have both acted it out and have experienced the after-results upon themselves. They have also experienced something of inner life, divested of the outer parts of mortality.

No elitist illusion must be admitted into the situation. This particular path offers its own opportunities. So do more earth-based ways of life. A professional sportsman needs and finds testing and taxing opportunities for aggression, discipline, and physical courage not at all needed for the tuning-in of inner sensibilities. His work gives him no access to these, but it is still a strenuous search for one kind of perfection. It is not for those on earth to claim superior or exceptional merit for their different footpath.

It is important, as has been seen, not to look at life after death as the aftermath of a completed story. Instead it brings consequences and opportunity; nor can there be a holding out of the hand for rewards. The most common cry of discarnates is: 'Now I see how much I still have to learn'. Whilst law reigns everywhere, as all accounts tell, the very idea of uniformity in the inner world is one born of human limitation. In the end, each makes a unique contribution however long it takes to find the way to it.

Meanwhile it is useless to try and bypass karma in order to replace it by our own false idea of what is holy. Holiness means wholeness; how can one be whole by side-stepping the very path intended to bring it about?

Undoubtedly a guide's picture of earth life is more sunny and bears a more serene aspect than our own. If a God-force exists behind the scenes, but in the result men have too often brought chaos to earth, then it needs to be accepted also that the God-force after all created the men

who brought the chaos about. Men are likely too to have the power and the duty to correct it. Guides usually teach that though free will is inviolable, it does not exist in as many areas as men are inclined to believe. No-one will deny that life at times can be inexorable. Consequences cannot be upset, but they can be worked through for better or worse. In terms of free will it is not the situation in which we find ourselves placed which is nearly so important as our reaction to it. In expressing free will in this way we gradually change ourselves and thus in time life on earth also. Just as a pupil's situation, or some of it, represents part of his past, his free will response is creating part of his future.

The early stages of teaching present what can easily be grasped; it is for immediate use. The inner part remains, suspended, inaudible, until pupils one by one can and do enter into that inner silence where it can be received. This calls for a growth in serenity, a growth usually needing very persevering cultivation. It will necessarily come and go in the early stages. For even when serenity is well established, much of the meaning still remains in the invisible – contained in the mind of the teacher as he watches over his flock – and cannot be commanded by the most attentive ear. It has to be awaited.

The 'moment' is therefore most important. It must be caught whilst it is offered. This requires an especial kind of readiness in the pupil. The tug upon his attention, of the most delicate kind, can arrive when he is least expecting it, or is engulfed in something else. But the pupil cannot say 'wait a moment'; if he does the slender thread becomes broken. At other times he can be ready and obedient, but the delicate etheric surround of his aura in which his antennae work, a little beyond and outside the physical level of attention, can be shattered in an instant by another earth person who knowingly or

unknowingly intrudes, or, more importantly, by an indulgent shifting of the listener's own attention from the inner back to the everyday outer.

The process of listening and then assimilating is often depicted as a still pool which reflects the sky. If the pool ripples, the image becomes distorted or disappears.

Using another set of terms, much of the personal part of the guide's teaching will represent a part of Karma-yoga, the path of one's own deeds. At other times the teaching will reflect Jnana-yoga, the yoga of intellectual concept, or Bhakti-yoga, that of devotion and worship of the God-force. The pupil must be ready for all these aspects, these roads within. It must be so, since as the pupil climbs the Jacob's Ladder, he is mounting towards where 'All is one' and 'All are one'. These lofty levels are first reflected many times at lower levels. A guide does not allow himself to be one-sided. If for instance he were to teach nothing but Karma-yoga the pupil would almost certainly become self-absorbed and therefore selfish, which in turn would create fresh karma. So every now and then the pupil is fanned by the guide with breezes from other climes. Appeal is made to other aspects in his own nature. Yet the strength of the teaching still lies in the simplicity with which it is given. The guide is not there to tie intellectual knots, he is far more interested in untying them.

4

Two opposed simplicities need to be recognised. The first lies within the very texture of the teaching; it is simple because guides have the skill of simplicity. The second sort is not true simplicity, but is the simplification preferred by humans who falsify the teaching by lowering

its interpretation, bringing to it what really belongs elsewhere. This is not a fact especial to this subject, it belongs everywhere in human teaching.

Some might suppose that the purpose of these inner teachers is to cut us down to size. On the contrary it is always to help us to enlarge ourselves. Such a task cannot come about overnight. To fall for the apparent glamour of being a bit better informed than one's neighbour needs to be avoided like the plague; it is a sure prescription for ignorance. True teaching in this field is always pointing to mystery. To recognise that one is placed upon a low step of the Jacob's Ladder is of considerable help. In this low place the teacher first brings what can best be described as a *showing*. He shows something of what in its fullness belongs to consciousness at a higher step; so he can only show in part, hint to us. Consciousness does not have the hard edges the mind likes to impose. This learning is not by precept, which is a static thing, but by insight which is a growing quality. Insight can be spoken of more truly as sight into inner things; in-tuition too is tuition from within and the very opposite of vague guessing.

Everyday man, seeking proprietary rights even for his own religion, only brings limitations by making exclusive claims. Nothing is easier than for the Ageless Wisdom similarly to be confined into a small box by claiming what a large box one's knowledge really is.

Western expressions of the Ageless Wisdom over the last hundred years through Theosophy, Spiritualism and Christian Science, have each become faulty, in the way humans make them faulty by simultaneously claiming too much for them, and at the same time bringing too little of them into their own breasts. According to occult teaching, it was planned that these three expressions should be implanted into human life at about the same time, close to the overlapping of the Piscean and Aquarian ages, in

order to offer facets of the Ageless Wisdom which could complement and illumine one another. The common impulse behind all three was to bring the inner spiritual factors in man into more open focus. The three presentations remain available for those who wish to ensoul them in ways more closely in tune with their original purpose. It may be asked: is not the Ageless Wisdom powerful enough to express itself so that these human confusions do not immediately result? But the Ageless Wisdom together with other spiritual outpourings, does not overcome human folly; that is for man himself to do.

> The value of the work ahead lies in the mental and spiritual fields, and the methods of mediumship will be brought into a completely fresh area. You will find more and more people attuned, and the continuation of our efforts to assist them to find themselves first, and then to find the God within afterwards, will help them to become mediums in their own right. . . . The awakening occasioned would be a dawning of the whole of mankind's consciousness, whether they be of high or low estate in their relative value to the God self and the God whole. We are aiming very high . . .[1]

5

A more general suffusion of teaching is also given, percolating directly to many individuals through their own private meditative focussing. This is both easier and harder than mediumistic receptivity. It is easier in that it does not call for mediumship's full dedication towards increase of sensitivity, to a degree which makes a medium's life hard to bear. The saying: 'Every man his own medium' does not mean that everybody will become a busybody handing round messages, a large number

doubtless both inappropriate and incorrect. It means that more and more men and women will learn how to develop their own spiritual lifeline of receptivity, not in selfish self-regard, but to see more truly. In any life, there will be much which it is necessary to work upon, an unweeded garden where the gardener is at first curiously unaware of the real weeds; telepathic instruction can point to these. It has its own resemblances to bringing some of the disciplines of the monastic spiritual life into private spiritual striving in the everyday world. Many of course already have the necessary sensitivity through finer than average tunings of their conscience. Yet as every monk needs a novice master and a confessor, and every chela needs a guru, so the discarnate teacher operates in a similar manner upon the tuned sensibility of the pupil. His method is one which the pupil finds to be as full of warm and tender insight and compassion, as it is of gentle firmness. A joy arises in recognising the inherent rightness of the insights produced. To established disciplines in the religious life, the results of this lay sensitivity will no doubt seem very elementary. However it gives an access of consciousness to many engaged in the mental tumult of daily life who might not otherwise find it, and who, as they improve their own tuning, will find just the material needed for their immediate private situation. It will also be free from any rigid theological encrustation. It can prove a very economical process for getting the right spiritual message to the right person at the right time.

6

A central purpose shared by guides is to bring a general re-assurance to those on earth. This they can only do if we

can see that their gaze includes a great deal that seems dark and evil. They have indeed experienced much; their authority – one which they never demand on their own account – is partly based on the enduring qualities of character which these mingled experiences, of light and dark, have bestowed. They acknowledge too other beings senior to themselves. What we are to them, they are to these senior beings; the junior is always in the care of a senior.

The guide overcomes the many separations which humans impose on themselves through his own qualities of loving. He loves as easily as he breathes; and his love renews its integrity through its individual insight. It is not a blanketing love, but perceptive in a way both piercing and tender. It offers support which the pupil often finds beyond his power to measure. The possibility of a creative partnership is presented between different spiritual levels, between his and those of his pupil, and also between the separate levels in the pupil himself, levels already awaiting his own work on himself. Constant human disappointment arises between what we see and half-intend, and what we actually achieve. This is especially true in a creative partnership where the stakes are higher than in everyday matters.

7

It is only rarely that the teacher will give a deeper glimpse of himself, an intimation of his real environment and his place in it. Nevertheless the hints come, brief and seldom though they are. Some of them relate to his own place in the chain of teaching. Sometimes he speaks openly, at other times his voice is more private.

It is not wrong to seek to find yourself, it is wrong, having found something of yourself, of your heights and depths, to forget the God force that can activate these. That is very important. All teaching has not to centralise on the individual, but to see what can arise out of the individual and find that central force which really is God. And if you stop and say, I have found my centre and do not identify it with a spiritual force, the God-spark, then there can be no good progression, but only an accumulation of knowledge. Spiritual wisdom has to stretch out like the sun-rays. The sun does not say: 'I will only shine on this one, I will not shine on that one', the sun says: 'Here I am, my light streams out and those who are ready to be bathed in it, let them accept it'. That is like the God truth.[2]

We so mingle and co-mingle in our world that at times it is difficult to differentiate and to become one personality . . . You must not worry about this, we are so interwoven, we are so much attuned when we speak in this way that if I speak with one voice, I may be speaking for many.[3]

We meet many wonderful people who are so advanced that they do not wish to be identified, they just come as one group of light and love.[4]

As you go further along this pathway in our world, although names are given, names are not important, there is a much greater unison of spirit and mind between the advanced ones. They no longer claim identity as identity and for identity.[5]

We speak as the intermediary, for the great ones do not speak.[6]

We take you towards the mystical where experience *is*, and one does not seek to analyse, one merely absorbs and becomes a part of the whole.[7]

I want you to lose sense of four walls, of a sky, of an earth. Pure spirit reaching out to pure spirit. There need be no prayers, there need be no supplications for protection. Our

motive is to find more of God. So we lose the things that we know, to find the reality we only glimpse. This we must attempt more and more in meditation.[8]

We are taken away from the things that relate to what you can hear, see and touch: we are just part of all, this is what we aspire to, this is what we search for – all the learning, all the wisdom, all the teaching leads ultimately to this one point where you can become identified and absorbed in the All.[9]

I must tell you of one of my inner experiences. I was taken by those who are wiser and brighter and I was enfolded with such love and such a feeling of being identified with and through the God force that I felt never again would I ponder and ask questions about things I did not fully understand until I was ready and able to assimilate them without questioning and querying, and it was as though I was taken on some wonderful experience, enfolded by those whom I saw not because their light was too great, and I was lifted and lifted until the light became so brilliant, that I could not bear more. I was told: 'just absorb without thinking', and I just became part of that unity, a tiny little spark of that wonderful source of light. I know not where I went but it was to one of the inner beings.[10]

I have come back from the inner kingdoms strengthened in mind and purpose. When I was allowed to glimpse into the inner kingdom I saw the light from the presence of the Great Ones – the brilliant light – and it is as though I was a child brought to my knees to see such beauty without any sound, just emanation of the spiritual quality in which I was allowed to bathe myself. I came away and I felt that everything about my person was bright and shining and I hope so much I can retain some of that illumination outside and inside.[11]

8

At a certain stage each pupil has to decide whether he will

allow information from this wider (and at first sight so intangible) background to play a vital role in the moral choices which make up his life style. Some things he accepts, others he chooses for the present to ignore. Between receiving and truly accepting, a considerable time lag often arises. Some parts of the picture will have already come alive in his daily living. Other parts can seem empty or useless encumbrances or just plain difficult. If he proclaims that he readily accepts all without making use of this regulative process from his own sensitivity then he is on course to erect yet another dogmatic prison around himself.

At times the pupil will wonder how much his guide knows of him. (There is also the problem that if the guide's view of the pupil differs from the pupil's own, which is the pupil going to accept?) The pupil recognises in time that, apart from insight in specific details, the guide is not overmuch concerned with daily details; what he holds is a creative vision of the essential self; qualities towards which the pupil is already slowly struggling, others which only show themselves to him as yet as a vague unease of which he has not discovered the source, and others, joyful creative ones which the guide speaks of, and which the pupil is just finding his own way to lay hold of.

At the same time the student cannot, and never can, look upon any spiritual quality, when it has been achieved, as his own. In a mysterious way he comes to know that part of it, though he appears to own it, is beyond his own being. Something larger is in him than the 'himself' he knows on earth, whether he calls this larger part his senior partner or his higher self, or looks upon it as the spark of God-force which lies within, which is him, and yet of which he can never be more than the servant. It is most necessary that he never allows himself to fall into any trap of inflation concerning it. In the spiritual realm there are no 'free gifts',

and yet everything is freely given. The worth, so far as earth is concerned, lies only in the use which is made of it.

What comes to, or is given to a student, can be looked upon as a contribution towards the deeply serious need for regeneration (re-generation) of earth life through countless individuals, and the prevention of destruction of our present civilisation. Even if he finds it hard to acknowledge, power to help the world is available to and through the individual. Only when it is consistently refused by the bulk of mankind is the stern necessity likely to arise of hard lessons of *apparent* destruction.

Truth is presented by spiritual beings in many-faceted and many-levelled ways, with no claim of monopoly for one type of teaching. What at first seems contradictory later is seen to be complementary. These levels gradually come to live together in the individual heart like good neighbours. A frequent cause of contradiction arises when one aspect is enlarged beyond its correct range. Tribal laws are right so long as they are recognised as being only tribal. Human equipment is simply not large enough to absorb full truth.

The presentation which guides can offer is therefore incomplete. It has to be. They hope to develop their presentation slowly into a fuller shape.

Meanwhile they present a general attitude into which they hope their earth pupils and others can gradually grow. It is one of receptive generosity to what life brings, a making full use of all it offers. Essential to this comes discipline towards the self, and of course service as a return for all that life has offered.

Man through experience, through suffering himself, learns to understand the sorrows and the needs of his brother-man. This is the simple truth. To get into the heart of each other, respecting each other's needs, whether they be spiritual, material or mental; and all men are different, so brothers

have to learn by love. Every man, woman and child you know or encounter needs something from you and it is for you, by your inner perception, to see what it is, what your gift should be, what it can be. Do they need your comfort, your material gift, your wise gentle guidance or your strength? What is it your brother needs? You have to find out and then give it whole-heartedly as Jesus the Christ gave it.[12]

No guide will ever save a pupil from disaster, if the results it brings are needed to achieve a larger purpose within him, or to fulfil part of the law of cause and effect. In short there cannot be any favouritism. Times arise when the pupil faces a dark episode; here as guides say, guide and pupil alike must bow before the spiritual law. All roads lead to a mystery large or small. That is part of the price for the loan to us of a few years of mortality. Here much of the mystery is not able to be unveiled. The guide leads the pupil towards accepting the burden of the mystery and recognising its presence. From his own higher step on the Jacob's Ladder it is a mystery also to him.

Then the guide is less often blamed by his pupil than in earlier days for what is really the pupil's own fault, or for difficult yet fruitful incidents brought for his learning. Since it is the spiritual law and not his own interests which the guide's life is serving, the guide's stature has gained through his serenity, good humour, loving attention and dedication. These qualities form the spiritual sunshine which gradually fructifies the humble pupil as also do the rains and storms which accost him, sometimes from his peers, sometimes from his own past, and sometimes perhaps brought purposefully by the teacher himself.

The torch can bring light, it can also sear and burn, and can also set fire to those things around you, so be very careful to whom you give truth and insight. The wise ones do not put

their words in long ways, they put them in simple ways but they have to be worked at.[13]

Whatever is learned on earth, or we think has been learned, the path still winds forward, the quest goes on. The horizons extend, not diminish. As the pupil achieves a measure of self-cleansing so, by his own growth guides are able to show themselves to him in ways which are a little nearer to their full being. The more truly the pupil casts himself away, and finds himself again in simplicity, the more fully he is able to know both teacher and the teaching, and himself also.

Sources of Quotations

1 to 11   From private teachings
12   White Eagle Lodge: a private teaching
13   A private teaching

D1613159